Life

Centering

with Breath & Awareness

Life

Centering™

with Breath & Awareness

A Step-by-Step Guide to

Self-Empowerment and Transformation

Ronald B. Wayman

West Jordan, UT 84088

ISBN: 978-1-947176-01-0

The material in this book is intended to provide overviews of research and information that may provide insights into your life. Any suggestions for techniques, treatments, or lifestyle changes referred to or implied in this book should be undertaken only with the guidance of a medical professional, therapist, or healthcare practitioner. The ideas, suggestions, and techniques in this book should not be used in place of professional advice.

Designed by Deborah Luke

Printed and bound in the United States of America
Published by Live by Heart, LLC
A subsidiary of Sensory Dynamics, LLC
8817 S Redwood Rd #C
West Jordan, UT 84088

Visit LivebyHeart.net or LifeCentering.com

*This book is dedicated
to my wife, Janette,
for her unending support
with this book and many others.*

Life

Centering™

with Breath & Awareness

is a part of the

Live by Heart™

Series

CONTENTS

PREFACE

My purpose centers on coaching and facilitating others in their quest for living a balanced, integrated, enjoyable, and focused life. Living a focused life can be an adventure when it is internally aligned between goals, the heart's desire, and peace, even down to the subconscious level.

I find great satisfaction in assisting others in their personal quests for the treasures of peace, success, fun, and joy. These are treasures meant for those who choose to stop believing the fears of the "false self", and who choose to discover the authentic or true self.

Discovering your own truth is important, adhering to it is profound. With the self-coaching techniques found within this book, you will receive insights and wisdom, learn to connect to your inner world, and facilitate personal healing through breathing, centering, and meditation techniques.

ACKNOWLEDGEMENTS

There are so many individuals that make a difference in one's life. One of those is my father. I have come to realize the value of my father's ability to become quiet and focused when he needed to find answers. This became significant to me later in my life. Before he died, I returned the favor when he started to release his inner fears after surviving a major heart attack. I was able to be a facilitator using breath, emotion, and understanding, allowing him to address, resolve and heal much of the emotions he had been carrying from the past. Thank you, Dad, for being a great example of integrity and inner connection to the divine. And thank you for submitting to my insights and allowing me to be there when you went through your struggles. Bless you on your journey.

I'm continually indebted to my long-suffering wife, Janette, who's support enables me to continue my work. I'm also appreciative of my colleagues, Tami Davis, Debbie Luke, and Jennifer Marie. They are so supportive and helpful with editing and graphics and many more tasks that cannot be mentioned here. They are true friends.

INTRODUCTION

The Heart and Mind of it All

Life Centering enables you to connect to the disparate parts of yourself that have been screaming to be integrated into your life. Only when the whole self is in alignment, can you create and form the life you desire.

Unfortunately, the path to success and joy is sabotaged by many things, including stress from work, bills, marriage, partnerships, relationships and negative beliefs that are stuck- rock solid in the mind and body. When was the last time you remember *not* being stressed over something? You simply look at the TV, read a newspaper, walk certain streets, visit particular schools, show up at work, attend church, drive the highways, listen to the radio or get a call on your telephone. In fact, it seems to be easier to be at stress than it is to be at peace.

We experience so many conflicts and stress in our daily lives, that few find the "Peace" they desire. They use forms of recreation, like watching movies, playing video games, traveling, or taking long drives in order to relax and de-stress. They often will use food or exercise to deal with conflicts. However, this *could* be a form of denial or avoidance. The feeling of stress relief is a great fix; however, for long term results, you'll need to address some of the core issues that you have been avoiding. This will clear the path toward that elusive sense of peace that you have been yearning for.

In truth, peace is easier than stress. Many people believe this, but do not know how to let go of stress in order to achieve peace and joy. This book will assist those in the mire of stress to find peace and assist those who have found some peace, a way to maintain it in spite of the storms of life.

Great change begins by small and simple means. So, take a few minutes to Center and do a daily meditation. In other words, "Just stop and take a breath!"

A Life Centering meditation is an integration of mind, heart, body, and soul. If you are on the path of integrating and centering yourself, then you can spontaneously experience moments of Joy. This means that you can confront the sorrows and disappointments of life in a balanced way.

Living life in a balanced way attracts others who are also integrated. However, if you are scattered, fearful, or angry, you could attract the opposite of peace; you could attract disintegration and disease. Sometimes, that which you attract is a reflection of a condition of a part of your inner self. It is possible to attract a wholeness of joy, passion, happiness and peace! Where do you start? You start within.

The procedures and processes presented herein can be used to create a perpetual source of centered support.

This book covers techniques of Breathing, Meditation, and Visualization combined with the deeper understandings of Intent, Gratitude, and Wisdom, taught in a format that is easy to understand and follow. There are several levels of techniques to choose from to support you in creating a peaceful and productive life. My desire is to empower you to access the

Divine energy that God has given each of us, in order to find the peace you are longing for.

The basics are quite simple:

- Stop.
- Listen.
- Put aside all your cares.
- Focus on the inner self.
- Focus on your heart, or your navel, or your feet.
- Connect to your discoveries.
- Nourish self.
- Breathe in.
- Breathe out slowly.
- Breathe in Life.
- Breathe out any burden.
- Pause.
- Repeat.

As you follow these simple and powerful processes, your inner self draws upon all your previous understandings – thus, beginning the process of connecting and integrating. Once you let go of all the silly stuff, clutter and inner noise that keeps you from the answers you are truly searching for, you may discover that your greatest source of truth is within you. This is the seed of God that has been gifted to every one of us. As the psalmist wrote, "Be still and know I am God." (Psalms 46:10)

There are many great centering techniques to be found in Yoga, Tai chi, Qigong, meditation, prayer and other spiritual practices, all of which you may follow with joy. If this is so, then why read this book? What makes this information worthwhile to you?

In this book are several modalities compiled in a form that is easy to use and can be put into action today. Also, there are a few new techniques that are simple and effective. The intent is that this collection, when used for only minutes a day, will integrate the various aspects of your being into one powerful and complete whole.

Complete wholeness will give you peace, joy, clarity, inner power, effortless living, spontaneous motivation, creativity, a sense of gratitude and forgiveness, open-ness and vitality. All you need to know in order to get started is included here in these pages. Combine these techniques with your desire, your intent and your essence, to create magic.

There are many terms used in this book that may be unfamiliar to the reader. Following, are some brief descriptions of the basic concepts of Life Centering.

Centering – *The action of alignment and integration of the mind, heart, body, and soul into a cohesive and flowing experience and State of Being.* The result of centering is a connection to the inner most parts of the Self so that the mind, heart, body, and soul are on the same path without internal conflict. Being centered feels like a calm river of energy flowing through the body, enlivening the soul, and connecting the heavens above to the earth below. When you are Centered, you are connected to your authentic Self, while also feeling connected to all other parts of the universe. It is a state of calm happiness. It is a place of Stillness. It is an "inner knowing."

Conflict – *The opposite of centering.* Conflict is the result of the mind, heart, and body manifesting different agendas and beliefs. It is as if different parts of your Self are at war and oppose each other. Conflict can manifest as explosive emotions or suppressed feelings that lead to confusion, frustration, anxiety, depression, illness, and/or disconnection with Self or others.

Self-talk - *The mental feedback that a person gives themselves throughout the day.* It is automatic and spontaneous. Often self-talk can be negative and destructive. Other times, it can be productive and supportive. It usually reflects the state of a person's inner world. When you are confident and calm, the self-talk tends to support that. When you are upset, angry, fearful, or lacking in self-confidence, then self-talk reflects negativity toward self or others. Authentic inner communication is powerful and uplifting. It opens an individual to new insights and awareness. Destructive self-talk creates mental ruts, shuts the truth down and negatively filters your view of life and others. "If-only", or "I wish" self-talk provides justifications for a person to live in a fantasy that does not have a happy ending.

Centered Breathing – *Breathing, moving, and meditating that assists you in bringing congruency and alignment of the mind, heart, body, and soul.* The purpose of centered breathing is to focus the attention of the mind to the act of breathing, and away from the clutter of thoughts and distractions. Centered Breathing increases oxygen and flow throughout the body and activates the parasympathetic, or Rest/Digest nervous system. This is the state of healing, and the way to align all the aspects of the Core Self.

Core Self – *The Core Self is a "still point", a quiet and peaceful state of being.* The Core Self is an active and alive state, although it is not an emotion, an object, an accomplishment, or an attitude. This centered state of Being is grounded in clarity, oneness, peace, strength, and confidence.

Alignment - *A synchronization of the energy patterns of the mind, heart, body and soul.* It is like the harmonizing of a song. The mind, heart, body, and soul each carry a unique energy pattern, or frequency. When they are synchronized, the multiple notes create harmony. When there is disharmony there is a misalignment, leading to internal confusion, or chaos. The act of centering allows conflicting beliefs, emotions, and memories to shift out of chaos and into congruency, bringing the person into a state where their energy can flow. This allows the individual to obtain a state of healing and oneness. Alignment allows a person to achieve optimal energy levels, as the entire system is working together. Living in disharmony and chaos requires the expenditure of energy to maintain the misaligned state.

Congruency - *A synchronization of the intentions and beliefs of the mind, heart, body and soul.* Often, there is a disagreement within a person's own system. The mind may think one way, but the emotions and/or body hold a different belief. This is the cause of many unexplained headaches, emotions, aches and pains. When a person is congruent with their belief and purpose, they are in alignment. Congruency of the heart, mind, body, and soul aligns the person's energy into synchronized patterns. This allows the whole Self to align to the same purpose, direction, and path.

Wholeness - *A Centered state where there is an alignment of the mind, heart, body, and soul.* The state of Wholeness brings with it a calm, natural flow and connectedness to one's own energy fields. Wholeness attracts spontaneous living and joy. This state of alignment relies on a matrix of communication between all parts and all dimensions of a person, simultaneously communicating and creating one beautiful symphony. A transformation into Wholeness brings all things into One, like a universe inside one's Self.

Attuning – *Tuning the chaos and randomness of the mind, heart, and body into a symphony that is blended and harmonious.* Opposing, or incongruent emotions and beliefs leads to internal conflict. Conflict can give rise to discomfort, illness, and emotional upset. Attuning brings into account the various agendas within an individual. Centering helps the body integrate the many parts of the Self into a harmonious state of Wholeness.

Mudras –*Hand or body positions that can hold and carry information.* Mudras are commonly used in yoga as well as in Energy Kinesiology. As demonstrated by the posture, body positions convey the state of a person. For example, sadness is displayed by holding the shoulders forward with the torso slumped, while feelings of confidence and courage are displayed with the shoulders back, the head upright and the torso straight. Hand mudras employ the placement of fingers and thumb in various positions. Each finger placement, as well as each postural position carries a specific piece of information, which is conveyed through the nervous system to the brain, the chakras, and other energy systems, supporting the emotions and body's energy fields. You can enhance centering with the use of mudras.

Knowingness – *An internal awareness.* A Knowing is a clear, intuitive observation of an understanding that comes without force or computation. It is simply an awareness of what is and what is not. When a person is centered, Knowingness or Knowing is easy and clear. Knowingness can come at any time, but to facilitate a deeper insightful state, seek to be centered and aligned internally. Knowingness allows you to attune your inner parts so that the information coming from the Core Self and the universe is concise and authentic, and of course, valid. Knowingness is a state of trust.

Grounding – *A connection to the earth that is physical, emotional, mental, and spiritual.* A tree needs its roots to be well established in the earth so that the rest of the tree can be abundant and thrive in the environment. Roots that are well grounded can feed the rest of the tree, and likewise, be fed. Like a tree, we receive energy and nurturance from the Earth. To be properly grounded the whole tree, and the whole person, needs to be aligned. The centering and aligning of all parts of the tree, or the person, to one energy pattern and purpose, assists in grounding through the roots as well as with the source of life energy. All bodies can experience the profound sense of life-force or the source of energy. It flows deep within and is facilitated with grounding and centering.

Source of energy – *The life-force energy that flows from nature.* This is known by many names, such as chi/qi, Ki, or prana. Every being inherits this energy at birth which fuels us until death. In the natural sciences of Eastern philosophy, there are several types of source energy that are identified. Source energy comes from parents, and is also derived from air, from food, from earth, and from heaven. Excess stress and misalignment of energy uses up source energy too quickly. Centering helps the body conserve this precious life-force or source of energy. Breathing in a centered way, or eating in a centered manner, improves the quality of life-force from the air and food so that the body can use it without difficulty, thus super-charging the body with energy. When you center to your core-self, to a still point, you can experience the magnitude of the original chi/qi or inherited life force and source energy. It is real, authentic, and truly precious.

Heart –*Through the Heart we connect to ourselves as well as to others.* The heart has different aspects: physical, emotional, mental and spiritual and energetic. The physical heart is vital to our physical existence, as it not only pumps the blood, but reads the blood to monitor our requirements. The emotional heart can break, and

8

it can heal. The mental heart can influence your mind and can give you passion to live in each and every moment.

The spiritual heart is close to God and the purpose of life and sharing. The chakra heart is an energy center that connects the unseen energy around us with the nerves and the brain. The brain heart is found on the right side of the brain, and is emotional and fluid in its processing, a place of dreams and music. The heart is an essential part of all aspects of life. Opening the closed heart creates great joy and may be repeated often until the centered heart chooses to remain in this more spontaneous way of living.

Navel – *The naval was the portal for nourishment while in the womb and continues to be a place for energy nourishment.* The navel is located in a central place in the human body. The naval carries great significance in Eastern Medicine. It is a bridge for the yin and yang, the opposing energies of the body. The navel is close to the lower "Dantian", a power center addressed by practitioners of Qi Gong, and holds strong life-force of energy in the lower portion of the body. The navel bridges this Dantian energy with the energy in the solar plexus and sacral chakra fields. It is one of the representations of Center.

Jill is a charming young lady. She exercises. She lifts weights and runs. She lives in an exciting city and has many friends and associates. But behind this seemingly beautiful life is a woman full of fear, fear of her compulsive behaviors, fear that others will find out about them, fear of success, fear of failure and fear of rejection. She was addicted to food, love and people's positive opinions. With some coaching, she saw

through the fog of her fears and was impressed with her true self or core essence. However, she could not get her focus off of her problems. She had to gradually start centering her life. She looked at her physical, emotional, mental and spiritual pain and saw how she sabotaged her life.

She examined those beliefs and emotions that were in conflict and fighting for position. What she saw was that a part of her desired space and time for quietude and self-care, while another part of her desired the fast-pace of a fighting-to-win lifestyle. She was able to resolve this by honoring all parts of herself. As she began to do the techniques in this book, she found that she was able to center herself "in the moment", and manage the stresses of life as they appeared, rather than avoid, suppress and escape from those less-agreeable parts of her experience. She found joy in the various aspects of her life and learned how to integrate them, thus, becoming more congruent in her daily living. She became "centered."

The techniques outlined in this book are designed to help people begin changing, re-centering and returning to the lives they really want. Start slow and easy with just five to ten minutes, and each day add a little more time. With just these few minutes a day, you can maintain and enhance your alignment and integrative process and empower your life.

You are invited to begin in this moment to

Return to Center.

CHAPTER ONE

A Centered Heart and Mind

Two Sides of the Brain

In order to understand how we are to integrate our mind, heart, body and soul, let us begin by looking at how the brain functions. The brain has a major division between the left and right sides. This division is not only physical, but functional. We process information using both sides, enabling balance and integration, but each side of the brain processes information in a unique way. [1]

The outer part of the brain, or the cortex, handles the conscious processing of information. These include your thoughts and decisions, as the cortex is responsible for cognitive thinking, long term memory, visual processing, and conscious commands for muscle function.

Let's address the two sides of the brain, in order to understand how we can better process information in a balanced and integrated way.

---

[1] The default is for each side of the brain is to function according to the left/right division; however, studies have shown that each side of the brain may have an ability to compensate when necessary to perform many of the functions of the other side of the brain. This is based upon brain lateralization research performed by Michael Gazzaniga and Roger Sperry.

A Comparison of Left and Right Side of the Brain Processing

Left	Right
Verbal	Nonverbal
Analysis	Synthesis
Details	Whole picture
Word Symbolic	Object Symbolic
Linear	Spatial
External Reality	Internal Reality
Holographic	Gestalt
Sequential	Random
Rational	Non-rational
Digital	Spatial
Logical	Intuitive
Linear thought	Holistic feeling
Structure	Experience
Mental	Kinesthetic
Vision and words	Vision and music

The Left Side

In general, the left cortex is associated with words and logic. It may be constantly calculating and organizing information as it analyzes and discerns details. It is compartmentalized, detail oriented and tends to be rigid. This is where we process math, science and reasoning. This is like the structure and order of a house.

The Right Side

On the other hand, the right cortex processes information with pictures. This is the seat of creativity, intuition and awareness. From the right side, we can see things as part of a bigger picture (gestalt) and we can be fluid and adaptable. Emotional processing is more dominant in the right side of the brain. This is like the décor, colors and furnishings in a house.

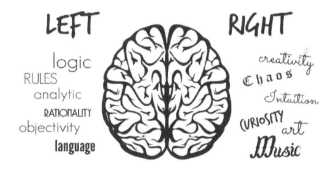

Conflicting Houses

Problems can arise if the functions of the brain get trapped in either the emotional side or the logical side. When the left and right brain are unbalanced, they are conflicting and warring houses. When it is unbalanced with left-side dominance, it becomes too analytical, and it justifies, denies and sabotages.

When the brain is right-side dominant, if combines with the heart to house the emotions of regret and depression. The brain may be integrated, but in an unhealthy, unbalanced way. This imbalance affects our ability to support a healthy mental/emotional life.

When the left and right brain are communicating and integrating, they create a peaceful, balanced state. When integrated, the brain can see the details as well as the overall view, in other words, the forest AND the trees.

Bridging the Two Sides of the Brain

Sometimes, when the left and right sides of the brain are not communicating well, internal conflict can arise. The results can be confusion, resentment, wishful thinking, rigid thinking, feelings of being lost, misunderstood, and/or a state of judging oneself or others too easily.

There has been much discussion in the past several years about ADD, ADHD, depression and other mind disorders. Often these are associated with the brain's inability to associate and communicate properly within itself across the major communication bridge of the brain: the corpus callosum.

The corpus callosum connects the left and right sides of the cortex as well as the left and right sides of the limbic brain.[2] The corpus callosum is the major bridge for logical and emotional information crossing between the left and the right sides of the brain.

This bridge is essential for integrating the responses to your daily experiences. The bridge has to deal with life's mixed bag of interpretations. For example, the bridge may function very well

---

[2] The limbic brain is also lateralized (two sided). Refer to the work of Paul MacLean.

at play or with some of your co-workers. However, if there were some past experiences that left some emotional pain: for instance, a divorce, firing, break-up, etc., then the processing of information is immediately inhibited when these memories are triggered.

You may become stuck on one side of the brain or the other. You can lose your ability to see reason, or you may suddenly feel a strong emotion that you don't understand. In that moment, you don't feel fully in control. It is as if the right and left sides of the brain are speaking two different languages. It is as if your reasoning ability has now been hijacked by your emotions.

When there is an emotional trigger, the brain will use the memories of the cortex, the limbic brain[3] and the brainstem[4] to recover the situation and possibly restore balance so that the bridge of the two sides of the cortex are talking and working together.

The cortex of the brain needs to be balanced to have clarity. Thus, if there is an unresolved trigger, the bridge will not be able to balance the two sides of your thinking - emotional and logical. What if life's triggers cause miscommunication through the bridge to happen more often than you'd like? When the two sides of yourself are in conflict or repelling each other, your ability to

---

[3] According to the triune model of diagramming the brain, the limbic area houses deeper emotional responses on the subconscious level.

[4] There is a 3rd part, which is referred to as the brainstem- the reptilian or primal brain. The primal brain is charge of breathing, sleeping, and automatic body functions. The emotions of the primal brain, including rage, fear, panic, freeze, and other unconscious responses, are there for protection and survival. The main brainstem responses we experience are Fight, Flight or Freeze. They are automatic, primal responses, yet can be controlled by the cortex, the Left and Right Brain. If a person is unable to modulate these strong reactions through their cortex, then they may manifest their primal emotions as "rage" or be a "reactor". The purpose of Life Centering is to assist you in learning to modulate your primal brain, so that you can enjoy life rather than react to it.

move smoothly through your daily life diminishes. This will cause delays or distortion in processing information, and most often, lead to errors in how you perceive your world. This course of thinking becomes reactive and leads to a variety of issues.

What if life's triggers cause miscommunication through the bridge to happen more often than you'd like? When the two sides of yourself are in conflict or repelling each other, your ability to process daily life diminishes. This will cause delays or distortion in processing information, and most often, lead to errors in how you perceive your world. This course of thinking becomes reactive and leads to a variety of issues.

When the mind is stuck on one side or the other during the learning process, this can cause problems with memory, analyzing and motivation. In relationships, this can cause misunderstandings, misgivings and misperceptions. In professions, this can lead to dismissal, loss of self-respect and mistrust of others.

What causes the two sides of the brain to lose integration? Often the cause can be traced to an emotional or physical trauma, genetics, accidents, allergies, etc. There are techniques that will help counteract these negative effects and help integrate the two sides of the brain. These techniques include emotional processing, deep breathing, guided imagery, meditation, prayer, reading of scriptural and inspirational text, walking outdoors in nature, sensory integration, nutritional support, energy balancing, brain integration, and stretching, which can all be done with the *Life Centering* techniques presented in this publication.

Centering & Integrating the Mind with the Heart

Emotions are processed at several levels in our brain: conscious, subconscious, and unconscious. The front part of the cortex, with its role in conscious thought, deals with emotions that arise when the bridge is having a great day. The subconscious and unconscious emotions are managed by deeper areas of the brain. In the triune brain model, these deeper levels are named the limbic and the brain stem areas.

The processing in the limbic area includes the functions of learning, clarity, autonomic functions, a sense of well-being, a sense of fear, a sense of anger, and the sense of seeking for food or adventure. Whether you are cold, hungry, wet, or afraid, the limbic brain is involved.

The emotional states that the limbic nuclei process are happy, sad, fear, anger and any other positive or negative feeling. Just like the cortex, the limbic area processes emotional information uniquely on each side. However, unlike the cortex, there is emotion on both sides, and some research has demonstrated that positive emotions will show up more on the left and negative emotions more on the right side of the limbic area.

Now, let us extend our view of the brain to include the heart. Often the brain represents the logic, and the heart represents the emotions. However, the heart's emotional state can be associated with the right cortex, as well as the limbic area. The heart represents feelings, and deep, subconscious storage of emotions.

The heart has long represented the energy of emotions, and it carries that energy in Western society. In Eastern society, the heart represents a deeper "knowing" or understanding of what is happening, thus; the right side of the brain represents the "heart" of understanding and experiencing emotional states.

The mind represents the left brain, the logical side of thinking, as well as thoughts and conscious choice for action.

The mind attempts to create internal alignment with "inner self-talk." These are internal discussions of why things happen, what should happen, self-doubts and self-appraisals. When there is difficulty "lining things up" then the brain cannot synchronize or align itself. In its attempt to create balance and harmony, the mind will engage in unproductive "self-talk" that becomes clutter to the mind and the heart. Often referred to as "monkey chatter", it becomes cyclic and problematic.

This monkey chatter pushes away peace and self-confidence and replaces it with feelings of not being good enough, not being love-able and not being capable, as well as a multitude of "shoulds" and "if onlys," (those "sticky", subtle regrets). The chatter can trigger your right-brain emotional side to overreact with sadness, fear, anger, etc.

Often the two sides of the brain do not integrate well because of *dis*integration between the heart and the mind.

What does it mean to have the mind and the heart integrated? It means they are in alignment, going the same direction. It means they are shaking hands and agreeing to go forward, together, side by side. It means there is no internal manipulation as can occur with mind control techniques.

There are many programs that advocate a strict control of the mind, in order to overcome your issues. These may work well for many people, but I advocate a different approach. Consider the benefits of honoring your whole self, body, heart and mind. When the heart is honored, rather than controlled, this is true integration.

Forcing or Flexing the Relationship

If there is a person in your life, including you, that is forcing their opinions or belief, causing stress to themselves or others, this indicates imbalance between the mind and the heart. This creates a huge energy drain. It takes a great deal of energy to force life and force ideas. Being at peace allows a person to enjoy life with greater flexibility and choice. The forceful mind requires more energy than the balanced mind and heart.

There is great benefit in being flexible and honoring your mind and your heart. However, when there are conflicts, this is an indication that you need to pay attention to your life. The conflicts and confusion of the self-talk can become destructive to a person's peace of mind, thus, reflecting chaotic energy to relationships and to other parts of their life.

Conflicts and confusion of the mind and heart are internal alarms. When an alarm goes off, you may not know the reason. For some, they attempt to rid themselves of the alarm by ignoring it. Others drown it out with addictions, activities, forced affirmations, substances, food, or emotional disconnections. Try allowing wisdom into your life. Start using the techniques in this book to open your heart and mind, learning a new way to balancing and center yourself. The answers will surface when your "inner-self" feels safe.

In many relationships, one person holds the energy of logic, analysis and justification - left brain energy. The other holds the energy of emotion, creativity and depression – right brain energy. With a little work, both partners can become complete within themselves, making the relationship whole.

Centering & Integrating the Body with the Mind & Heart

The chatter referred to earlier can also trigger the body to have somatic, or physical reactions. Itching, pain, sweating, coldness, tightness, pounding heart, and fatigue, are some of the somatic reactions that you may sense when there is a conflict. Sometimes the body is just "hot and tired." However, there is usually an emotional component to most sensory experiences.

There is a connection between your thoughts, feelings and the sensations in your body. This is the mind/body connection, but of course, right in the middle of this, is the heart. The heart tries to bring understanding to life and its problems. The mind is trying to logically put all the pieces together. But, when the body reacts, and the heart and mind are not working together, logic is illusive.

The third part of the triune brain is the brain stem. This primal area, along with the limbic area, is unconscious, and responsible for the sensory reactions of the body. Any spontaneous body reaction is primal in nature and is one of the alarms when there is conflict with the heart and mind.[5]

The body also responds to excessive unresolved issues. We hold our issues in our tissues. The physical body retains positive and negative emotions. From the viewpoint of Chinese medicine, the emotions, or "climates" of life - cold (fear), or heat (anger), can get stuck in the cellular structures of the organs. For example, the liver holds determination and anger. When the heart and mind are integrated, negative emotions like anger will not be retained when the emotions are released appropriately.

Regardless of what emotions are stored and where they are stored, the heart will be affected. Thus, you could call this association, the heart/body. When there is a problem, the amount of energy stored in the heart/body is greater than the amount of energy stored in the mind/body.

If you truly have the desire to move forward, working with the heart is paramount. Centering is one of the best ways to begin, and to continue the process of releasing deep-seated emotions and beliefs and is a powerful tool for integrating the mind and the heart. It is self-empowering.

---

5 Refer to the Glossary at the end of the book for the definitions of Mind/ Heart, Heart/Body, and Mind/Body.

Considering Resistance

We need some resistance in our lives. With no resistance, there would be no need to change or grow, and we would not acquire wisdom in the process. Bringing balance into your life would not be possible without imbalance. Centering would not be possible unless there was resistance or opposition to being centered.

However, as you push against stress, run away from opposition, fear conflict and resist the resistance, your reactions become more stressful and burdensome. You create walls and more problems that compound the original stressful situations. Most often the resistance will either make you become more aggressive or passive—but not more balanced. You have become your own enemy.

The idea of centering is a balancing act. When you are in that balance, you are capable of changing a flood of commotion to a simple flow, to transform a tornado into a breeze, a tsunami to a soft wave on the beach. Individuals from all walks of life: jumpy business people, anxious moms, disillusioned teenagers and children with scattered minds, have one common problem - their own misalignment, misperception and fear keep them from being balanced and centered.

How do you create that balance? The goal of the meditations and breathing contained in this book is to create the capacity to flow *with* the energy of the emotion, the pain, or however the energy is manifesting. It could be emotionally or physically based. It could be painful or full of bliss. Energy is just energy. The judgment we apply to it creates the stress. The idea is to learn to smoothly breath the energy in and out like the flowing tide of the ocean.

Through the breath, you can reduce the resistance you have to what you are feeling. Your body does not hold a judgement to your emotion or pain. To your body, it's just energy that needs to be processed. Energy that can be moved through the breath.

Many of the martial arts, in particular Aikido and Tai Chi, focus on drawing the "chi" (life force) of the attacker and gently redirecting it. Thus, not only do you divert power from the enemy, but you empower yourself. If the enemy is your negative internal beliefs, mind-monkey chatter or emotions of the heart, you can show the body how to re-direct the energy. You take the damned-up energy and give it a path, a stream to flow to the ocean and start anew.

Mike was a hard-working union boss who was determined to negotiate whatever "the guys" needed and enjoying the prestige this garnered for him. In fact, he really enjoyed the conflict and winning the battles. But, over time, he started to notice that he had only brief moments of satisfaction, but no joy. The fights became more painful to him, whether he won or not. His body was in pain and had deep inner conflict.

He was always on guard, as he had been since he was a child, wary of any possible attack. He was not living; he was ready for death or to "kill". A nice guy that was all tied up inside. Mike was coached to let his guard down. His guard was based on resistance. His resistance was founded in fear; fear of his ex-wife, his boss and his mother. When he finally saw that they were actually afraid of him and that they could be a help to his quest of peace, centering and integration, he started to relax, ever so slowly.

Mike found some of the hidden messages embedded in the resistance. He realized that his mother wanted him to be a strong male who respected women. His mother tried to force him to respect her; in return, he had seen her as a "shrew." He saw his ex-wife as a manipulator and covert thief, until he gained an understanding that she, also, was helping him learn how to be a strong male and to respect a woman whether she was angry, upset, nice or not.

When he started respecting his ex-wife, despite his previous negative view, she was treated with calmer conversations. It took a few events before it started to happen spontaneously, but it did. Eventually, even while others in his relationships were in contention, he was able to be clear minded and at peace.

Opposition is powerful only when you give it your power. When you see the messages hidden behind the opposition, emotionally and spiritually, they can liberate you. This principle applies in all aspects and areas of your life. All your experiences can assist you in your quest.

Resistance can be a signal of inner stress and fear, both physical and/or emotional. Address the resistance like the matador does, flow it through your red cape. Continue to internally pass and process the bull of resistance until you embrace the negative energy and transform that energy into a form that supports and honors the self.

Attuning the Parts

Centering involves all aspects of your life. By using breathing, visuals, music, affirmations, emotions and other tools, the body can release the internal struggle and return to center. You are helping the body communicate at levels that you shut down long ago. To assist your quest, it is helpful to have understanding and awareness of some of the major areas that you are aligning in your being.

Centering and integrating the right and left sides of the brain with the heart, mind and body means that you are tuning the various parts of your being to communicate with each other, within each system and between the systems. As you go through the following techniques, become aware of the Level at which your thoughts and feelings are flowing.

To begin with, consider the physical, emotional, mental and spiritual areas. For example, if you are feeling physical pain, then you are focusing at the physical Level. You can ask yourself "where is the pain?" Focus on this pain area with deep attention. Use one of the centering breath techniques from this book to send calm energy to that pain area. However, when you are on the physical plane, you are not really aligning the emotional Level directly.

In the list below are some ideas for the four areas of awareness to identify where you are in life, enabling your choice of going to the next level of centering.

What Level Are You Experiencing?	
Body (Physical)	Body sensations of pain, hunger, calmness, breath, temperature, etc. in your organs, body parts and physical environment.
Heart (Emotional)	Feelings, emotions (warm or cold), passions and desires tagged with emotions. (Check in with feelings to verify their validity, do the feelings match the experience?)
Mind (Mental)	Thoughts, analysis, discernment, logic, integration of thoughts and feelings, questions and judgments. (Check in with logic and understanding to verify the validity of the experience).
Soul (Spiritual)	Awareness of the parts, purpose, mission, integration of thoughts, feelings and soul. Gratitude, flowing with the divine, universal and personal path.

Here is an example of finding and seeing your Level through meditation:

Jane was scattered, fearful, angry, moving so fast with "to-dos" and slowing down so much with fatigue, that she was lost in a fog. She was so overwhelmed, and she did not realize it. Somehow the fog was pierced and she took the suggestion of meditation. Within a few weeks her young son Tom commented how glad he was that she was meditating. She had not even realized he had noticed. He told her,

"You're calm now, Mom." That statement brought an awareness of the effect her stress had upon her children. She saw how much her children were changing by her private meditative actions. Several years later, she is still grateful.

As you consider where you are coming from, realize that each part—right brain, left brain, heart, mind and body—is important. There is no part that is more or less important than another. The key lies in balancing all the separate parts into one great whole. For example, if someone is in the mind excessively, it doesn't mean they are above the emotional plane and that they need not dwell there at all.

In fact, this denial of emotions is a major obstacle to spiritual enlightenment and true centering of the mind, heart and soul. Many "analytical types" say that emotions make a person a victim—and emotions do, if that is a person's main focus and if they are ruled by them. But balanced emotions enable a person to not only experience the fullness of life but empowers them to create and enjoy the great abundance of life and live in all the Levels and possibilities.

Be aware of the Levels in all areas of your life, particularly when performing the centering techniques. Choose to balance yourself. Practice the techniques over time to enhance your awareness. Over time your awareness will grow and bring you further wisdom, healing, alignment and balance. You will have a greater understanding of yourself.

Benefits

There are benefits to focusing on these techniques on a daily basis. Centering and grounding in all areas of your life will lead to tremendous health benefits, great awareness, spiritual experiences and emotional freedom.

Achieve peace, joy, health, clarity, focus, passion and power

❖ Manage stress

❖ Gain new insights of your internal landscape

❖ Communicate with the inner self

❖ Recognize the lies to self and any sabotaging

❖ Enable yourself to change the sabotage

❖ Empower yourself with simple techniques that you can use in your daily life

❖ Enable yourself to focus in the moment

❖ Propel forward through lifes challenges

❖ Create the future, clean up the past and experience the moment

When you choose to use these centering techniques, you not only integrate and align your inner self, but you become more empowered in the moment you need it. When stress arises in your life, you can focus on the solution. If you are not centered, there is a tendency for more anxiety, scattering, blaming and pain. Lack of focus of the heart, mind and soul can support self-delusions. Convergence of heart, mind and soul will support a focus on reality.

If you have sabotages that create roadblocks to calming your inner self, these roadblocks will set up personal, family and other emotional stories that are intensified with fear, anger, resentments and sadness. Centering allows for false beliefs, negative emotions and physical toxins to surface. Once they surface you have a chance to clear and transform them. The more you align yourself, the harder it is to hold on to the sabotages that could embed themselves deep within your inner core.

Three types of Meditation

In the November 2014 edition of Scientific American, an article called "Mind of the Meditator," gives an interesting view of contemplative experience; in other words, centering, breathing and meditation. They considered three types of contemplative experience and then related it to the areas of the brain that appeared to be most active when viewed through neuroimaging and similar mapping technologies.

The three mentioned are "Focused Attention", "Mindfulness," and "Compassion and/or Loving Kindness." The meditations and centering exercises of this book include these aspects of the contemplative experience.

Focused attention

Focused attention focuses on one object, a concept, or the in & out of the breath. This is helpful for all of us who sometimes have a wandering mind and need a way to come back home to ground zero and re-focus on calmly breathing and centering.

Focused attention brings the brain back into a centered state. Part of the Default Mode Network in your brain stays active even when you are not. Many of the techniques in this book begin by having you notice your breathing or creating a visualization.

Mindfulness

Mindfulness brings awareness to your mind, heart, and body. It helps you to reconnect yourself to your sensory body. While some individuals are able to sense many parts of their body, others may not, and experience overactive thinking and racing minds. The purpose of Mindfulness is to bring acute knowing and attention to the scattered thoughts, random sensations, and multiple feelings that channel through your body and mind throughout the day.

Mindfulness helps calm anxiety and depression. It taps into many systems in the body, including the cardiovascular, digestive, and neurological systems, and helps to align your body with your mind. Centering with mindfulness is found in many Life Centering techniques. It is used interchangeably with focused attention in the centering techniques and breathing exercises.

Compassion, Loving Kindness & the Brain

The concepts of Compassion and Loving Kindness have been brought into the mainstream by Spiritual leaders like the Dalai Lama. At the core of Buddhism and at the basis of Judeo/Christian/Islam religious practice is the concept and intention to send love and kindness to others. Even the originators of the philosophy of stoicism taught love and compassion.

Compassion can bring physical and emotional benefits. The nervous systems of the body calm when a person is filled with compassion. In the article, it states that even neurology is affected. Specifically, compassion brings unity to the temporoparietal junction in the cortex of the brain.

This area of the brain also processes emotional signals. For instance, compassion leads to empathy, and empathy activates the cingulate gyrus. This brain area is overactive in those who are highly sensitive when making decisions and when dealing with internal moral conflicts. It is under-active in those who lack any empathy at all. Thus, compassion meditations can bring peace, calmness and a reduction in anxiety for many.

I find great peace when offering an unconditional state of compassion to people regardless of their condition. You may increase your own sense of alignment and peace by doing the Life Centering techniques with a feeling of compassion for others. Realize that everyone you meet has a message to share in some form and that it is a blessing to serve and share with the "one human family" that inhabits this beautiful God given earth.

No one is isolated. All of us breathe and share the gifts of air, light, fire, water, wood, and earth. Focus on the breath, awareness and mindfulness, and share the universal gift of life through compassionate meditation and loving service.

Where and When to Use these Techniques

When? Anytime. The optimum schedule is three times a day: once upon rising in the morning, once during the day and once before going to bed at night.

Where? Nearly anywhere. The simple centering techniques can be used at home or work. Though the deep meditative techniques are better done in the privacy of your own space, you can use the simple ones while driving, exercising, even while communicating with others.

Warning: The life force, or "chi," that is created by doing these techniques is very powerful, so the environment and thought processes you engender will have deep and lasting effect. Be wise to make sure you create the environment, thoughts and feelings you want to reinforce.

Take your time. You don't have to hyperventilate. Hyperventilating is not the intent here, for that could cause some physical and emotional discomfort due to possible excessive toxin release. Enjoy the techniques. If your muscles grow sore, drink lots of water and place your hands, palms down, on the sore area for four minutes. If you grow dizzy, drink lots of water and put your hands on your kidneys for four minutes (palms of the hands on the lower back). Hold the bottoms of your feet. Breathe slowly, methodically and deeply. An Epsom salts footbath can also help. Drink an herbal tea of chamomile, spearmint or lavender.

Unresolved emotional issues can arise. Just as physical toxins have an opportunity to finally make an exit, so too can emotional toxins be released that have been physically blocked. Breathe through them. Honor them. If you fear any emotional releases you could sabotage your process and re-store them in your body. Honor them by letting go. You learned so much by your life experience and now your release will give great relief to your physical, emotional and mental body. Drink plenty of both physical and spiritual water at times like these.

Eventually your body will adjust to the procedures and actually get a fantastic high. Instead of craving harmful substances or debilitating behaviors, your body will begin to desire the fruit of centering. You will start to love simple things and enjoy life.

Bon Appetite.

Return to center and savor the centered life.

CHAPTER TWO

Centering Through Breath

Notice how you are breathing. Is your breath high in the chest or lower in the abdomen? High in the chest will cause the body to tighten more, receive less oxygen, create more mind chatter, more dehydration, more tight muscles, more concern and more anxiety. Shallow breathing is the most common breath for Westerners because of stressful lifestyles. It can represent a fear of letting life in fully or a fear of letting go. So, do an experiment: take a breath, then let out all the air. Do not breathe in any new air. After a few moments watch your body tense up. The mind focuses on one need. Relax and breathe normally.

Two-thirds of the oxygen intake and two-thirds of the blood vessels lie in the bottom one-third of the lungs. When your breathing is shallow, parts of the lower lungs and aspects of your spiritual/emotional self, feel this strain. Notice how after doing this exercise you automatically breathe deeper and easier. Notice that your life energy in your body is flowing and your mind is clear and light.

Breathing from the abdomen and lower part of the lungs will cause the body to take in more oxygen and expel more carbon dioxide. It will initiate neurotransmitters that will cause less concern, less mentalizing and less chatter in the mind.

Dehydration, muscle tension and tightness will decrease. Deep breathing will ground the body and release the soul to experience spiritual freedom of expression during the breath. The deeper the breath, the more the whole body is nourished.

Attaining a centered life is achieved only through the breath.

Beginning Techniques

The following two techniques are very similar. They help connect the parts of yourself that normally are ignored in Western culture, i.e., emotions, feelings, body and spirituality. This is excellent for stress reduction and inner nourishment; both are needed to balance busy lifestyles.

The first technique focuses on the heart and is easier for most Westerners. It provides immediate results for stress relief and clarity of mind. There are individuals who use this technique to lower blood pressure. The second technique, Navel centering, is good to start practicing at night. It helps ground or calm the entire body to a full relaxation and a sense of complete connection within. You can be strong and rooted like a tree by focusing and centering through the Lower Dan Tian. It is an energy point from Chinese Qigong that resides just below the navel. If your personal life is scattered and topsy-turvy, try the navel centering technique.

The intent is to bring in life energy, or chi. Let the life energy flow throughout the body at all levels and exit with any toxins. Repeat again, bringing newness of life and exiting with old. To keep the stream of life freely flowing, use some of the centering techniques.

Heart Centering (Western style)

Take a deep cleansing breath. With the exhale, send out stagnant energy and open up for fresh new energy. A deep cleansing breath is one in which you breathe deeply, from the bottom of your lungs to the top, filling your entire chest and belly with air. Put your hand on your abdomen and start to inhale by having your abdomen move up first. Use deep cleansing breaths to clear out any surface blockages.

1. Focus on your heart. Sense and feel the beat of the heart. (See Suggestions).

2. Take a deep breath through your nostrils. Pause your breath for a several seconds.

3. Staying focused on the heart, slowly breathe out through your mouth (with the mouth in a soft oval shape).

4. Breathe in. Slow down your in-breath. Breathe in through your nose and pause your breath.

5. Stay focused on the heart. Clear the mind. Clear the heart.

6. Slowly breathe out through the mouth with the mouth in a soft oval shape.

7. Pause

8. Repeat again several times for several minutes a day as often as desired.

Suggestions:

❖ Notice your heart.

❖ Feel its physical parts, its emotional and spiritual aspects.

❖ Breathe OUT any and all trauma, misgivings, regret, resentment, sadness, hopelessness, blockages, sluggishness, fear, doubt and pain.

❖ Breathe IN life, freshness, spring, summer, hope, faith, love, compassion for self, calm and peace.

❖ Your breathing should be soft and light so that you would not blow a candle out if it were near.

❖ Do heart centering in the morning upon rising, during the day to calm yourself when stressed and in the evening to rest from your day.

Allow yourself to experiment with this technique; breathe in through the nose and out through the mouth. Then try doing the complete technique only through the nose, both in and out. The energy is reserved and enhanced with the nostril only method; however, more toxic energy (physical and emotional) is released with the nose/mouth combination.

Navel Centering (Eastern style)

Take a deep cleansing breath.

Exhale stagnant energy and create space for fresh, new energy.

1. Focus on your Lower Dan Tian (its entry point is just below the navel).

2. Sense and feel the vibration of the chi, the life force.

3. Take a deep breath through your nostrils. Hold your breath for 15 seconds or longer.

4. Stayed focused on the Lower Dan Tian and slowly breathe out through your mouth (with the tongue touching the upper palate while the mouth is in a soft smile).

5. Slowly inhale through your nose and hold your breath.

6. Stay focused on the Lower Dan Tian. Clear the mind.

Clear the Sacral Plexus Chakra (the energy field just under the navel – extending to the sides and back) continue to stay focused on the Lower Dan Tian.

7. Slowly breathe out through the mouth with the tongue on the palate, with mouth in a soft smile shape.

8. Repeat again several times for several minutes a day as often as desired.

Suggestions: The Navel Centering technique is powerful for grounding. Use it to handle scattering, fear, disillusionment, confusion, disassociation, confrontation and anxiety. An option is to clear other chakra energy fields (see the Rainbow Colors Centering in Chapter Three) or consider using this same technique on the Middle Dan Tian (Solar Plexus-Upper Abdominal region) or the Upper Dan Tian (3rd Eye – between the eyes).

Grounding the energies will bring a sense of peace and strength. Several years ago, an Aikido master demonstrated to the author at a group setting that despite his small stature he could withstand several people trying to tip him over. He centered his energy deep within the Lower Dan Tian and his focus went deep within the earth. No one in the group was able to move the little big man.

Imagery Techniques

You can do imagery and visualization meditations with centered breathing. Imagery will access the parts of your brain that are blocked from your analytical mind. Accessing these areas of the brain through imagery facilitates healing and centering because the doors of these areas open into the subconscious mind, where our beliefs and programming are stored.

Jean was in the last stages of healing her breast cancer. She had already tried medicine and some complementary healing modalities. Breathing huge sighs of relief, Jean realized she was going to live. However, she was still battling an ex-husband, which for her seemed worse than the cancer. In addition, she felt some problems near her ovaries and colon. She went inward and visualized redness in her colon. As she went through the visualization, she realized her constipated colon and the redness were connected to the feelings she had for her ex-husband.

She communicated with the redness and felt that it was trying to remove her resentment of her ex-husband but was stuck. After breathing through some of her resentment and redness, she was able to visually soften and move the redness and then bring it into a bright light to heal. During this process, she calmed her mind, heart and body to align to the understanding and purpose of his problems. This experience released an emotional block to her ex-husband and physically the blocked energy of the colon seemed to vanish. Her colon started to get well.

Visualization is a powerful healing and centering tool. Imagery enhances affirmations, pain relief, emotional release, centering, deep spiritual introspection, healing, clearing thoughts and intensifying intentions.

Here are some possible visualizations:

o   Trees (going through the cycle of life)

o   Water (waterfalls, rivers, lakes, drops of water, ocean waves, the sand with the waves washing ashore.)

o   Flowers (going through seasons of life)

o   Body, organs and cells (movement, change, nourishment, release of toxins, cooperation, regeneration)

o   Prosperity   centering   (visualize   path,   creation, assimilation, building, completion, fruition)

The following sections provide some sample meditations for imagery centering. Feel free to use these or other meditations of your own choosing.

Water Meditation

One of the more enjoyable meditations for centering is the usage of water. Water represents so many aspects of life and the earth. One of the main areas is emotional. The ocean of emotion seems to be tumultuous these days for most people.

Direct the energy in your favor, use water imagery as a way to calm down, thus calming the emotions that are normally rippling with undertow and high waves. Become calm and send soft strength to the inner self, bringing back the original watery sense of nourishment and creation.

The major component of the body is water. The fetus is enclosed in a watery paradise. Water is next to oxygen in importance for human life. Water imagery with centered breath is soothing and regenerating.

Though this meditation can be used with any of the centering techniques, it seems to be most powerful when combined with the nostril breathing and navel centering techniques, with emphasis on the kidneys. For example, during a centering technique visualize water flowing through the kidneys and lower back.

Imagine being in a peaceful place in nature. Imagine a beautiful stream flowing through a forest. Imagine the stream forming a winding river. Imagine the river flowing over an edge, creating a beautiful waterfall. Imagine being in the flow of the waterfall and breathing in the mist. Feel the water rush over your head, the shoulders and back. See the mists create multiple prisms of rainbow colors. Imagine the water flowing through your veins, into the organs and muscles and down to mother earth.

Option:

❖ Find a stress in your life. Visualize and feel that stress.

❖ Breathe out the stress.

❖ Breathe in the water   washing the stress free and away.

❖ Then, follow the water as in the water visualization.

Heart Centering with Visualization

The use of visualizations and imagery can be so relaxing, you might forget what you were so stressed about. This is especially true when you are focusing on your heart while doing the visualization. Earlier, the heart meditation was introduced. Now, try including some relaxing images with the meditation.

I remember hearing of a study that compared the effects of plants in the office setting. The study included offices with live plants, offices with artificial plants, and offices with no plants. The study measured stress levels of the employees in the various settings. The conclusions were interesting. The employees in the offices with no plants whatsoever showed the highest stress levels. The employees in the offices with either live or artificial plants showed less stress. Although actual plants have additional benefits, even the suggestion of plants, in the form of a visualization can create a powerful calming effect in our minds and hearts. Thus, introducing to your mind images of nature can be very effective at helping the nervous system to calm the heart.

As mentioned in chapter one, the fight or flight response is caused by the sympathetic nervous system. Of course, this is only in response to how most people live their lives. The fight or flight response is a reaction due to stressful messages from your body and mind. Optimally, one of the cranial nerves, the vagus nerve, then activates the parasympathetic nervous system, sending messages back down to the body to calm the heart and the other organs.

We can activate the parasympathetic nervous system by visualizing palm trees, islands, calm waters, clouds, majestic mountains, or beautiful flowers in a meadow. The images you choose should have pleasant associations for you. These are held in your memory bank. It is the associated, peaceful memories that activate the parasympathetic nervous system to send calming messages to the heart and the other organs.

1. Take a deep cleansing breath.

2. Touch and notice your heart (or another organ that you choose to support).

3. Focus on your heart. Sense and feel the beat of the heart.

4. Breath slowly through your nostrils while focusing on the heart.

5. Now imagine a scene in nature that brings you bliss or tranquility. Let the scene of the ocean or the mountain stream, or whatever you desire, play out in your mind. Imagine that your heart starts beating to the rhythm of the ocean wave or the wind as it sways the upper leaves of the palm tree or forest trees.

6. Allow your focus to include both the heart and the visualization, slowly continue to breath.

7. Imagine the water or air flowing through the body and moving with your body rhythm. Just like the nervous system, the body can respond to this movement of imagery and change discordant stress into calm rhythms. (There is always a rhythm to life. You can choose yours if you want to. Or, it will be chosen for you).

8. Stay focused on the heart. Clear the mind. Clear the heart.

9. Slowly inhale and then exhale.

10. Pause.

11. Gather the imagery and observe where it leads you within your heart and mind.

12. Pause.

13. Repeat again several times for several minutes a day as often as desired.

14. Allow the body a "breather", a moment of rest before another busy day.

Centering in the Moment

After practicing one of the heart centering or the navel centering techniques, practice the centering-in-the-moment technique. This is a powerful tool which may be used while driving, while in public or when waking up in the middle of the night. The key to centering is being present in the moment. Fear and other negative emotions are a result of living in the past or the future. *The magic always happens in the moment.* Alignment and peace are always found in the moment. Life can only be lived in the moment.

Harry experienced several traumatic situations that were causing inner turmoil. The external events were beyond Harry's control as his father and others close to him had serious physical and medical conditions. He is a personal trainer and has many communication skills and tools. However, he found he was ineffective while he was non-aligned. It compromised his integrity. He made matters worse for others when he was not focused and centered. He struggled internally until he realized that while he was not able to control other people's environments, he could offer relief to himself.

He chose to center and align to his inner self, his real self. He decided that instead of experiencing stress or worry that brings no satisfaction, only pain, indigestion and anxiety, he would center in the moment—

and the experience was fantastic, offering relief, clarity, focus and freshness. The newness it gave cleared his mind, heart and physiology. At that point, he became clear so he was able to assist his family and friends.

Life Centering always clears the mind and heart, heals the body and soul and often can create the space for others to be at peace.

You do not have to store sticky, negative emotions. When you are centered, the emotion of the moment is calm and clean.

Technique:

1. Stop

2. Take notice of your awareness state (Am I stressed? Fatigued? Overwhelmed? Anxious? Worried? Jumpy? Angry? Fearful?)

3. Notice your emotional state and focus on your heart.

4. Breathe new air and life into your heart.

5. Breathe out tension (breathe out both physical and emotional stress and tension).

6. Breathe into your heart:

   a. joy

   b. a place of joy or pleasure

   c. or any emotion or thought you desire – calm, gratitude, peace, acknowledgment or a positive affirmation.

Grounding Technique

A fun exercise is to get a partner and face each other while standing two to three feet apart. Gently push on the shoulder of the other person and see if you can bend them. Now, have them think of a stress and push again. Next, have them focus on their Lower Dan Tian (the area right below their navel) and push again. You will notice a big difference between the three options.

Most people are the easiest to bend while thinking of a stress and the hardest to bend while focusing on the Lower Dan Tian or on the feet. Your natural state before stress is to be "grounded" – that is the energy that is balanced at the center of the body. Your body functions so much better when you are grounded. You think more clearly. You feel better. You are more in tune with the inner soul.

Many individuals in Western culture live outside the reality of their true self. Instead, they live in a dialogue: "I have so much to do. I'll never get everything done. What should I cook for dinner? Why should I even cook dinner - the kids probably won't like it? I have to finish that project. I should register for the class. If I had taken the class last year I would not be in this trouble. I can't stand it when the kids don't clean up. I had to clean up the messes when I was young. I even clean up the messes for everyone at work. How come no one cleans up for themselves? Slobs. Even my boss is a slob. And why doesn't he tell me he appreciates the extra work I do? In fact, why doesn't he tell me more, period? Oh, I just hate that gossipy no-gooder secretary across the hall. I just don't..."

This inner dialogue may not resemble yours. Yours might be worse or it might be minor in comparison. No matter the severity, this is the monkey chatter in the mind, mentioned earlier. The chatter can come and go in a minute or last for hours, but the devastation to the integrity of the self-alignment is beyond words. Most people live with past self-criticism playing in their mind, like a worn-out recording. Imagine a life without the mind chatter, without the baggage and chains of constant inner nagging. This inner nagger can be *calmed* using centering and grounding techniques.

Grounding was hard for Karen. She did not want to be shallow and guarded in her relationships and communications, but she was afraid of personal pain if she was not accepted. Part of the problem was the lack of the full expression and experience of life. She had a hard time really enjoying relationships. She felt lonely, even among people. She often was scattered and had a hard time focusing while communicating and staying on task. When she began to follow these techniques, she found that her focus and clarity were enhanced. She started to become aware of life, her mind, the chatter, and how to breathe to transform the chatter into calmness and silence. As she started to feel and to become real inside, her fear lessened.

The following technique is simple but effective for releasing monkey chatter, if practiced often. Use the visualizations with any of the centering techniques.

1. Think of your chatter or your stress.

2. Now send your energy and …

3. … focus on your feet.

4. Imagine warming the bottoms of your feet.

5. Imagine that roots start growing from your feet into the earth.

6. Breathe in nourishment through the roots.

7. Bring the nourishment up into the body.

8. Breathe out toxins, releasing them to the air. Simultaneously imagine toxins being sent to the earth to change and transform into fertilizer for the use and benefit of all.

9. Feel the fresh earth through your feet. Become grounded and nourished.

Noise, Noise, Noise Everywhere

Yes, there is a rattle, a rustling, a rumbling, a yell, a sigh, a crunch, a creak and a click. The more you focus and become aware, the more you will notice that life is very noisy. In fact, the brain is so good at buffering the noises, that it produces a chemical and an internal procedure that creates a "false noise." When you hear a noise and it is repeated several times, the brain memorizes this noise, copies it, sends the imitation and shuts down the real input, allowing the body to use less energy. This also protects you from massive sensory impact and processing overload. Pretty ingenious, don't you think?

Mothers understand this concept because they have experienced their child being able to shut out their voice, yet the child still hears other noises around them. Maybe the child does not like the sound and pitch of the upset, nagging mother's voice. The child now tunes out much of his/her environment (the mother's voice). He is not really present. This type of filtering is not centering but is escaping and denial. It will not bring peace, but frustration to both child and mother.

For true integration and centering, you want to be aware of real sensory messages, not fake ones. And more importantly, as you center, you will automatically become more aware of the noise. When you can distinguish real messages, you will next learn to filter out the noise properly for true centering. (You have more control of the mind when you are dealing with the real sensory information, instead of the duplicated false information).

After the mind and body can move past the external noises, the mind starts noticing the internal noises of the monkey chatter. The chatter seems to be loudest when the body is quiet. Chatter is taking negative words and spreading them all over like oil. The chatter even takes on personalities, becoming a doer, a doubter, a whiner, a critic, a dictator or a pleaser. Most of the time, the chatter is a self-victimizer, like an internal parent verbally beating an inner child. The chatter thinks it has to be active to be appreciated and to really perform its job.

But you are not the chatter. You are not the doubter or any of those other performers inside. You are "me, myself and I." Those three are about all you can handle. In fact, the real you is more powerful than all those internal negative performers combined.

Use the centering techniques in this book and other meditation methods to handle the chatter and to silence or *calm* the noise within the mind and body.

Calming the Mind

The mind's chatter is most common when there is a fear deep inside that your sub-conscious is hiding from you. It sends a message to the brain to do the "noise-thing" as a distraction. The brain sends messages to the mind to talk and make noise. The hard part is to *calm* the mind. If the sub-conscious is afraid to deal with the possible revelation, the *calming* techniques often fail.

In that case, there are still things you can do. Replace your anger, resistance and opposition with understanding, integration and gratitude. Know that you can flow through the resistive energy of the fearful parts of yourself and work with your body when there is chatter and noise. Face your fear, go into it, feel it, go through it and you will be empowered. Be patient.

Linda was a sensitive woman with intelligence and intuition. Her sensory sensitivity sometimes made her body and mind react in a negative way, so her subconscious created a diversion with mind chatter. Linda learned to recognize the times of intense chatter—that show up as fear, doubt, criticism of self and sometimes others—as a signal that her body was hiding something. She would get mad at herself about such awareness, but now she connects through some of these centering techniques and meditation to that fearful part of herself. She coaches and supports herself to be safe rather than attacking and re-creating the problem.

She breathes deeply. Whether or not she can cognitively recognize the problem, she relaxes her body and consciously reassures her mind and heart. She uses the following Calming the Mind Meditation:

"I can trust." "I can be fine." "I am safe." "I let myself relax." "This is recuperation time." "There is nothing to do right now but relax." "There is nothing to worry about right now." "There is nothing but breathing and re-creating newness within." "Everything will take care of itself." While saying these affirmations, she used one of the centering breathing techniques in the book. She breathed out the negative thoughts and breathed in the new positive affirmations.

Saying these types of affirmations while in a calm breathing state will assist if sincerely offered and not forced. Often you need to feel the fear or the emotion and choose to expel it on "the out-breath." The focus on the feeling gives the body a pathway for those beliefs and fears to surface and be expelled. *Often the problem is not the fear but the lack of a path for its completion.* Consider the meditation as "the path" to assist you in flowing the fears through and out of the body.

If the fear and chatter continue, choose to go to the creative space of the mind and brain and create a story around the chatter and let it play out for a while as you continue the breathing and meditation. The creative space of the mind is the door into the Alpha space. The alpha frequency is the door to deeper states of consciousness.

It is okay when the body does not cooperate and continues to create chatter and noise. The persistent nature of the chatter is indicative of the level of deep concern of the inner self. Try using visualizations and take your mind on a trip to resolve itself.

When in this situation use the *nostril breath* technique (discussed later) to start the centering meditation. The brain loves the wonderful direct oxygen. When you flow that energy through the body, the mind will calm down. You may enjoy coloring the centering, which focuses the mind on the visual field instead of the chatter. Refer to the rainbow centering technique.

If you still hear chatter, use other centering techniques, such as counting the out-breath until you are relaxed and not in the mind anymore. Use a candle and focus on the flame. State an affirmation and let it resonate with the in-breath throughout your body, mind and heart. (The affirmation technique discusses this further.) A mantra with a sound vibration, is effective due to the repetitive nature and also because certain sounds have been shown to have deep healing power on those who are centered and aligned.

If you use a sound in a centering technique to assist the process, pick a sound from the appropriate sounds relating to the Law of Five Elements in traditional Chinese Medicine and their respective organs. Focus the energy of the breath in the respective organ or flow the sound and the breath into the body. (Also, imagine the associated color of the organ).

Category	Wood	Fire	Earth	Air/Metal	Water
Organ/ Yin	Liver	Heart, Pericardium	Spleen, Pancreas	Lungs	Kidneys
Organ/ Yang	Gall Bladder	Small Intestines, Endocrine Glands, (Adrenals, Thyroid, Pituitary)	Stomach	Large Intestines	Urinary Bladder
Color -Energetic	Green	Red	Yellow	Blue / White	Lavender / Black
Sound	Shhhh	Heeee	Ommm, or Aumm	Sssss	Whooo

The most common sounds are "Om-m", "Aum" or "Ong". They are delivered from the depth of the abdomen, with calmness in the out-breath. These sounds can be found in many native religions around the world and many people hear these primal sounds when they cover their ears and listen within or when they listen to a seashell held up to their ear. "Om is the sound nature makes when it is pleased with itself," wrote mythologist Joseph Campbell.

To recap the possibilities of *calming* the mind:

1. Acknowledge the chatter.

2. Flow with the noise. Give it a path to leave.

3. Work with the chatter.

4. Use affirmations of reassurance.

5. Feel the emotions and fear and give it a path to resolve.

6. Visualize color, a nature scene or create a story about the chatter.

7. Create a mantra (sound/affirmation coming from you).

8. Hear a sound (coming from outside yourself, music, tones or notes).

9. Count.

10. Focus on a candle flame.

11. Focus on the breath.

12. Use the nostril breathing centering technique.

13. Be creative.

14. Process the chatter with the emotional centering technique.

15. Feel the gratitude.

Silencing the Mind

After the chatter is calmed, the body allows the possibility of silencing the mind. If you start the meditative process by forcing yourself to silence your mind immediately, that will empower your mind to be noisier. The mind is like a child. If you push that child away without helping it mature, the mind-child will scream and holler. You may fight harder for calm and silence because you feel that you are not enlightened enough or did not do it correctly.

The goal is not always silence; the goal is to be aligned at all levels of experience. Sometimes enlightenment will take you to silence, inner joy, travels of imagination, physical well-being, emotional healing, or phenomenal breakthroughs of understanding. It is the transcending of the chatter and then the integration of the self with the inner self that leads to the adventure.

In reality, the mind is a wonderful thing. When the mind is your friend, and not the enemy, the adventure is fulfilling, not burdensome. First, calm the mind with the centering techniques and then it will be easy to flow into silence; a silence that holds more bliss than can be described with words.

Thus, work at calming, then silencing. Enjoy the techniques. Consider starting with the following technique, which is a great bridge to calm the mind.

Single Nostril Breath

This is a favorite technique for initiating entrance into a more relaxed state. Once learned, you can do it while driving or traveling, or at the beginning of a centering technique. Some prefer this technique throughout their sessions. You will find this is very powerful for brain integration.

Your body is designed to alternatively breathe more dominantly out of one nostril than the other. Every 90 minutes, your body automatically switches the dominant nostril for breathing. At the same time, the body switches which side of the brain is the dominant side to receive and send energy. This technique, also known as Nadi Shodhana, enhances and honors the body's natural integrative methods and power.

Technique:

1. Take a deep cleansing breath. With the exhale, send out stagnant energy and allow for fresh new energy.

2. Focus on your Lower Dan Tian (the point just below the navel). Sense and feel the vibration of the Lower Dan Tian.

3. Put your index and middle fingers down toward the palm on your left hand, so that the thumb, the ring finger and the little finger are extended.

4. Hold the left nostril closed with the thumb of the left hand.

5. Breathe *in* slowly through the right nostril.

6. Hold the breath for 10 seconds. (Later with practice – more than 25 seconds).

7. Focus on the path of the breath flowing through the left brain integrating with the right brain. (See or sense the breath traveling through your head and/or body).

8. Release the thumb and hold the right nostril closed with the ring finger and little finger of the left hand.

9. Slowly breathe *out* through the left nostril.

10. Pause for a few moments.

11. Slowly breathe *in* the left nostril.

12. Hold the breath several seconds (as long as you can stay in the flow).

13. Focus on the path of the breath flowing through the right brain integrating with the left brain.

14. Release the ring and little fingers and hold the left nostril closed with the thumb.

15. Calmly breathe *out* through the right nostril.

16. Pause.

17. Calmly breathe *in* through the right nostril.

18. Pause several seconds.

19. Release the thumb. Hold the right nostril closed with the ring and little fingers.

20. Breathe *out* through the left nostril.

21. Pause.

22. Breathe *in* through the left nostril.

23. Pause.

24. Continue alternating between the two for several minutes.

25. Focus on the breath and stillness.

The hand mode described above is called Vishnu. It connects Heaven and Earth and is very grounding. An alternative finger positioning that substitutes the pinky finger for the ring finger offers a lighter and calmer alternative. This mudra is called Creation/Destruction w/Heaven, and is performed in the same manner as the procedure above.

Play with both finger positions, and use the one that resonates with you.

Suggestions:

o   Do not push your breath or hold your breath for too long. The flight or fight nervous system is activated when you are forcing air or too desperate for breath. This breath should be natural and floating to be effective. Flight or fight breath is not grounding. Naturally focused breath should be very grounding and calming. Do not hold the breath so long that you gasp for air. You could hyperventilate, which means you are holding onto carbon-dioxide (a toxin) and you will not be grounding and centering.

o Breathe in with the flow of your own life experience. Create and extend the breath each time, which enables you to stay in the flow of your experience.

o Pause rather than hold. Pause a moment in time, reflect in the moment. Many hold onto past emotional issues, making it difficult to receive and experience new life. Breath means "life" and/or "spirit."

o Experiment with either hand for optimal results. Also, with the other hand, you may hold the palm up with the thumb and index finger touching, the other fingers extended. Refer to the section of hand modes later in the book.

o If there is tightness in your abdomen consider the following sections in this book: abdominal stretching, tightening the muscles or emotional centering.

Sleep Calming Technique

Insomnia is a very common issue. The anxiety many of us experience during the day produces so much adrenaline in the system that the body creates biochemical changes so it never has a chance to completely rest. For individuals in stress, the Flight/Fight system is always on alert, and the Rest/Digest system is repressed or exhausted.

When the body tries to switch on the relaxing and rejuvenating Rest/Digest system, there are too many mixed signals from your body chemistry, your mind and heart, that the flight/fight system continues without stopping.

Stress affects the functions of the organs and glands. For example, in the small and large intestines, stress causes toxins that set off chemical reactions leading to a disruption of hormonal balance, which can disrupt synchronization of the circadian rhythms of the body. Those rhythms, if disrupted, can keep a person awake and/or make sleep erratic and uncomfortable.

Sleep is important for health. If you are not getting restful sleep, there is a gradual buildup of toxins that will cause other symptoms. Ironically, these toxins and symptoms also cause or add to sleep disorders. Sleep allows the body time and space to cleanse and regenerate. Proper cleansing and regeneration support a centered life.

Larry was in constant pain. He was bent over and on his "bad" days had to use a cane. The author noticed that Larry's desire to be centered and calm was inhibited by all his physical symptoms. So, Larry started to drink 2 quarts of water a day, sought assistance to cleanse his colon, emotionally processed some of the hidden causes and received some energy treatments to relieve pain.

He used some of the breathing techniques for pain and to calm himself during the long nights. Within a short time, his constant pain became frequent. He started to sleep for longer periods of time. His frequent pain was reduced as he nutritionally supported himself and remembered to meditate and center morning and night. He saw that as his sleep became longer and deeper his health improved dramatically.

Larry was reminded that the last fifteen minutes before bed are the most important for sleep. Whatever you think about, stress about or worry about, will stick with you as an imprint for the night. Insomnia is indicative that the "lung" energy is too high, which means the body does not transition well to change.

The body is in a subtle panic and needs to stay alert and thinking, thus, not letting the conscious portion of the mind shut down at night. As you sleep, the thalamus nucleus in the brain turns "off" the cortex (consciousness) so that the body can focus on healing and regenerating. However, if you are too mental, then the thalamus determines that you must be awake to handle your problems during the night, as if it were day.

The subconscious is more qualified at integrating, solving, and regenerating without the interference of a busy mind. Quieting the mind before bed is a gift for your subconscious. Centering and deep breathing before sleep creates health of mind, body and soul.

Technique:

1. Start with the *single nostril breathing* technique.

2. After a few minutes, you can move to the Navel centering (Lower Dan Tian) or the Heart centering technique while breathing through your nose.

3. Move your focus to your toes. With each breath, send and receive calm energy through the toes.

4. Relax the toes.

5. Focus on your feet. With each breath send and receive calm and soothing energy through your feet.

6. Imagine the feet in softness.

7. Focus on your ankles. Do the centering breath.

8. Focus on your calves. Do the centering breath.

9. Follow in sequence up the body, gradually calming, silencing and soothing the entire body.

10. Continue to breathe and soothe the calves, knees, legs, hips, abdomen, chest, hands, arms, shoulders, neck, face, forehead and the entire body.

11. If you are still awake, then while doing slow centering breath - hold the palms of your hands on the outside of the jaw for two to three minutes. Place them over the Masseter muscle. This is the major jaw muscle responsible for the majority of the chewing action. Your hands should cover the sides of your jaw, underneath your cheeks, over the part of your jaw that hinges.

12. Put your palms on the sides of the skull above the ears (over the Temporalis muscle).

13. Put your palms on either side of the navel covering the lower abdominal muscles.

14. While doing this, return to the imagery of focusing on the feet up to the head, releasing trapped energy and calming the body.

Most people are asleep before they get to the hips. If you continue to stay awake, consider taking time during the day to be alone and center yourself with any of these techniques. Especially do the centering at times of stress. One creative and powerful time is a corresponding time during the day. For example: If the sleeplessness is around 3 am, then try some centering work around 2:30 to 3:30 in the afternoon for several days and see what happens.

Having a trust for life allows for deep sleep and is essential to deep spiritual living. Without trust, life becomes mundane or anxious, overwhelming or prideful. With trust, life is magical. With trust, life is supported, leading to joy.

Imagery for Centered Sleep

Imagine many hands of angels all around your body as you lie on your bed, supporting you, holding you in a state of peace and hope. Relax and give them your physical body. Surrender and let them take care of you throughout the night. Let your body, mind and heart float on this cloud of angels and enjoy the bliss of full support and ethereal nourishment.

The Living Breath & LITE

Most people only notice how they are breathing when their lungs are constricted. In truth, breathing is much more important to your well-being than any other physical activity, even eating. However, most people are so focused on their problems that they spin and spin in those problems and how to fix themselves with pills, thrills, and meals.

Many people who find their way to meditation practices are still attempting to push themselves into a perfect state of bliss, without really connecting to a natural way of breathing and living.

I have discovered a way of breathing that is an effective, more natural way of moving unwanted energy, while helping the mind and body become more centered and balanced.

I call it the Living Breath LITE program. LITE stands for Light Interval Training Exercise. The full program includes specific intervals for breathing, walking, eating, running, thinking, exercising and more. The most powerful technique is for breathing. It quickly and easily allows the mind and body to become more relaxed and centered.

The Living Breath interval is especially important because it is applicable to all those who want to be more centered in their meditations. It is effective for those who care to live "naturally" rather than "push" to live.

The idea is to help the body relax into the breath so that it helps "entrain" (go with the flow, so to speak) with the body rather than attempt to force the body into relaxation.

The intervals consist of repetitions and lengths of breath. The sequence and the number of repetitions is just as important as the breath itself. Do the sequence with a positive intention and watch your life change and time become more available. Time is like water in a river. Holding onto it will only damn up your experience. Let it flow with direction, understanding and joy, and time will become your friend.

You will be breathing in and out through your nostrils.

The Living Breath

Start with a **cleansing breath.**

- Next, is **one Short breath.**

- Now do **seven Long, slow breaths.**

- Then, breathe **five Medium length breaths**. The medium breath is the average between the short and the long.

- **Repeat this sequence 3 times.**

Allow the breath to rise and fall like the waves in the ocean. Unforced, calm and easy. The transitions between each breath and each type of breath are smooth.

You may use your fingers to count the number of breaths or mentally do the counting. The number of breaths is important, unless you are worried and "fret" about it. Relax into your counting. The act of counting can add to the calming effect of the practice if you allow the counting to aid you in focusing your attention. It can help you ease the scattered brain into a clear and focused mind.

The speed and time of the breath is important, because this will determine the type of energy that the nerves will respond to. The long, slow speed will activate more of the parasympathetic system.

The medium time and speed will encourage the entire nervous system to work together.

If you use a rapid breath to activate the sympathetic nervous system, it is not as safe nor effective as a neutral short breath. The short breath that is not too quick will gently activate Flight or Fight. The excessive use of the Fire Breath can increase stress for many individuals. I suggest the calm short breath which activates areas of the lungs that are sensitive to the stress system.

Note that most of the breathing technique is designed to support the parasympathetic nervous system with the long, slow breath. The medium, slow breath is a bridge between the two systems.

Both nervous systems are necessary. Sometimes when you are trying to force away the stress system, it does the opposite. I have found many people who are more stressed because they are constantly worrying about being stressed and anxious. Stress about stress is worse than the original stress. So, let yourself activate the stress system naturally and move out of it naturally. Both nervous systems are essential for daily living. All processes of the body require access to both the sympathetic and parasympathetic systems, however, whether your stress is physical, emotional or mental, the Centered Way requires a working balance between the two nervous systems.

The intention that you have is also very important. If even the thought of this procedure causes you stress, then please don't force yourself. But, if you will allow yourself just a few moments to follow the procedure, you will find that your mind will calm, and the excessive thoughts of "I don't have the time," or "I have so much to do that there is no time for this breathing stuff" will diminish.

Not having time to stop and breathe is precisely the cause of most persons overwhelm and confusion. When you are a puppet on the strings of overwhelm, your time is lost, the mind confused, your body heavy with strange pains and feelings, and your heart is excessively concerned.

The Living Breath will bring more living to a plastic, upside-down, crazy world. A Natural Life that is centered and balanced is worth living. Take back your life and your mind, and by the way, your heart too.

For more information, please see the LITE links found on LivebyHeart.net.

The magic is always in the moment.

CHAPTER THREE

Centering for Abundance

The joy of creating abundance is about more than just money. The centered feelings surrounding prosperity bring you to a state of calm and excitement, *not* a state of anxiety, panic, jealousy, control, resentment, manipulation, or revenge. Centered prosperity is one in which the world benefits from your prosperity and you benefit from theirs. It is a mutual force for positive growth.

Our negative emotional beliefs provide substantial motivation. These beliefs are usually fear-based. While it is difficult to let go of these powerful motivating forces, realize that the fruit of these negative forces is usually bittersweet and short lived; because the fruit creates cravings within that will only cause you to perform more while providing little lasting satisfaction.

With the centered approach, seeds of abundance and prosperity are planted with positive emotions. They are planted with the intent of empowerment for self, others, God and the universe. It is the easier path. It is much more difficult to create abundance and hold onto it comfortably in a fear-based negative state. It is a much easier to create prosperity when we are full of clarity, peace and purpose, and contributing to the higher good of all.

Creation Centering Part One: Intent

The process of Creation coming just from the mind is like a forced wish. In order to manifest an idea; you must add the heart to the process. This allows you to create the desire of your heart and mind together, a combination of deep intent with faith and trust. This is accomplished through expressing the desire to God, the Universe and the part of you that is divine.

Think, Feel and Visualize your deep intent, imagine sending it to the Universe or God and trust that the desired result will return. Hold the understanding that it is (a) in God's will, (b) for the benefit of all humankind and (c) for one-self's benefit.

Be very clear about what it is that you desire. The clearer you are, the more likely you will see the fruition of your desire. Clarity brings power to the act of creation. Clarity enhances passion, passion enhances life, life is eternal, eternity starts with purpose and purpose is clarity.

1. Do one of the basic centering techniques.

2. Upon exhaling, wait. Pause.

3. In your mind and in your heart, create your inner desire.

4. Focus on your creation.

5. Breathe in slowly. Pause.

6. Focus on the result. See the fruit.

7. Breathe out slowly. Pause.

8. Refocus on your creation, the passion, the desire and the intent.

9. Breathe in slowly. Pause.

10. Focus on the fruit, the result and the associated feelings.

11. Repeat for several minutes.

Use the power of intent to your advantage. When intent is focused, it can be like a laser beam. Intent can rally the electromagnetic energy within the body to trumpet messages of change within. Be aware of the power of intent, use it for the benefit of all and see how you can abundantly transform your life.

Abundance and Prosperity Centering

Using a positive, centered approach will serve like a magnet, attracting those people who are necessary in achieving your beneficial goals, be it the success of a business or other worthy ventures.

In all the breathing and centering techniques, use your abundance and prosperity intents. Some of the intents include:

All things work for my good.

Money easily flows to me.

My work benefits the world and my family.

I create a better world while earning income.

People come to me who want to make me successful.

I attract clients that want to empower their life with my services.

I attract substantial funds that I use for my benefit and the benefit of my family, my community, my world, the universe and God.

I am clear and on purpose with my finances.

I live my purpose in all areas of my life, including my work.

I am abundant and prosperous all the days of my life.

I enjoy associating with others who are seeking abundance and empowerment.

I am congruent with making money.

I am safe with lots of money.

Money is not evil.

Money is a gift to create a better life for all those who choose abundance and prosperity.

Abundance is creating fullness, joy and sharing in all areas of life.

I am worthy of my prosperity.

I Center with my True Self.

I am Centered and Balanced in all aspects of my life.

I Empower Life.

These are some sample affirmations and intents that you can use in the many centering techniques in this book. For many, their beliefs surrounding money create obstacles and frustrations. Some believe money is bad or evil. Others believe they are not worthy or good enough. These beliefs are based on past associations with painful emotional traumas.

If you choose to hold onto events as truth of your character, then you will struggle. But if you choose to learn from those events and change those beliefs to universal truths, then you will be successful. Start changing these old painful beliefs to abundant beliefs of "I am worthy," "I am good enough," "Money is Good," "Money is a gift for exchanging services," etc.

To truly change those beliefs, you need to follow the techniques in this book with a focus on the abundance issues. However, sometimes the issues are deeply set within the body as well as the mind. Thus, for additional help on emotions and beliefs, refer to the *Emotional Processing and Centering* section in this book.

Creation Centering Part Two: Obstacles

The power behind creation is not difficult to access if you are centered and at peace inside. Once there is an alignment of heart and mind, your emotions are the super-jets, the passion that drives the creation past the subtle sabotages that will arise. Emotion and passion are the super chargers to all creation activities.

Whether negative or positive, emotions will accentuate and accelerate your creation process. When you desire change, you will direct your passion in a positive way and will see your life transform abundantly.

Creation is a powerful force that continues every single moment - in your body, in the world and in the universe. As part of an ongoing cycle, if there is something being formed, there is something else being destroyed or dissolving. This cycle causes resistance. Resistance is a natural balancer in the universe, allowing change and creation. Without resistance, there would be no progress and no movement, only stagnation.

A kite flies in the wind because it is going against the current. Symbolically, if a kite demanded complete control and rebelled against the current, it would break apart and fall. A kite that finds equilibrium with the opposing current and has a desire to sail high, creates a fine balance in the air. This enables success. Even geese will use some resistance to propel them forward, but they take turns absorbing the opposing energy at the lead, to enable others in the flock to recharge.

See the resistance as a benefit, a way to strengthen and enhance growth. Consider a tree that is opposed by the wind. The bold oak tree absorbs the wind, growing stronger. The timid weeping willow tree has a much more difficult time and in a major storm is likely to break.

Do one of the basic centering techniques.

1. Experience the desire, the want and the creation.

2. Breathe in. Pause.

3. Experience the obstacles, the resistance and the pain.

4. Breathe out. Pause.

5. Experience the growth from the resistance and the effect it has on the creation.

6. Breathe in. Pause.

7. Re-experience any other obstacle, resistance or pain with new awareness.

8. Breathe out. Pause.

9. Experience new growth due to resistance.

10. Breathe in.

11. Continue for several minutes.

Creation Centering and Sensory Expression

In order to enhance your ability to create, learning to involve your physical body senses will expand and deepen your experience. Each human life begins with sensory experiences; thus, each person is equipped to relate to the sensations of the body. Use what God and nature have already given to you to create deep and lasting health, abundance and satisfaction.

1. Do one of the basic centering techniques.

2. Experience the desire, the want and the creation. Use as many of the senses as possible – smell, taste, touch, color, visualize, feel, hear, motion and intuition. (Even use different yoga positions as desired).

3. Breathe in. Pause.

4. Experience the obstacles, the resistance and the pain.

5. Breathe out. Pause.

6. Experience the growth from the resistance and the effect it has on the creation. Use the senses.

7. Breathe in. Pause.

8. Re-experience any other obstacle, resistance and pain with new awareness.

9. Breathe out. Pause.

10. Experience new growth due to resistance.

11. Breathe in.

12. Continue for several minutes.

The sensory experience challenges the obstacles, enabling you to understand the body from a new perspective. Sensory experiences during centering are not the ultimate design, but are often necessary for breaking through deep seated sabotages. Everything you experience is filtered through the sensory experiences you had as a child. Thus, many of your negative behaviors and dysfunctional thinking can be traced to sensory experiences that were not integrated when you were young.

Use this procedure to let the sensory parts, sight, sound, motion, body sensation, smell, etc. to arise, release and find resolution and completion.

Furthermore, a substantial amount of intuition is experienced in the Parietal region of the cortex of the brain, located in the upper posterior area. The Parietal region is also the sensory integration area of the brain. Thus, connecting to the sensory part of your brain and body will enhance and refine your intuition.

Sometimes, during the sensory centering process, the subconscious will enliven memories of pain or resistance. So, reconsider the power of resistance. It may seem like a revolution. It is. It's an internal revolution. Sometimes when you want to change your life, a part of yourself does not want to change. That resistant part wants to stay the same, not change or alter.

The intent of that resistive part is to keep you stable and heading down your accustomed, rutted path. If you keep going in the direction you are headed, you will keep getting the same results. Look at the resistance as a quality check – a reminder to be sure you are on the path that you really want to be on. Honor the internal resistance.

The degree of respect you give to the internal resistance is the degree of cooperation you will eventually receive back when there is transformation. Resistance creates the process for an evolution of balanced solutions.

Most people cannot imagine honoring the internal resistance. Why not? It can provide the reason to produce and create precious personality traits of strength, determination, intuition, insight, awareness, compassion, understanding, wisdom, goals, inspiration and integration. Resistance is a gift.

Question and Answer Centering

Deep breathing opens up the body and the mind to fresh possibilities, enabling you to find answers to some of your unanswered questions. There are several levels of this technique. The first level is more mental. This is a good level to see what kind of questions you are asking and to modify those questions to be more concise and clear. Remember, clarity is Power.

Be bold in your questioning. If you do not ask, how can the desire or yearning be satisfied? Whether the question is for deep spiritual meaning, healing an illness, praying for someone, financial concerns or abundant desires, let the questions be asked with full intent and trust. Sometimes the question will be answered immediately.

Most often the answers will come to you spontaneously while performing other tasks, while doing some automatic functions of life. These epiphanies are pieces of candy for those who ask. Watch for the magic of Question and Answer Centering.

Technique:

1. Do one of the basic centering techniques.

2. Clear the mind. Clear the heart. Clear the Lower Dan Tian (just below the navel).

3. Breathe in. Breathe out.

4. Ask the question. *Use clarity of questioning. Rather than "why me?" questions, (i.e. "Why am I in pain?", or "Why don't things work out for me?"), try asking questions that*

will help you learn the purpose behind the pain, (i.e. "Help me understand why I create this pain." or "Help me understand why I'm so frustrated.").

5. Breathe in. Pause.

6. Allow for the answer.

7. Breathe out. Pause.

8. If there is an answer, then ask – how will that change my life or situation? Or, what will be the consequences? Or, what will be the benefits?

9. Continue the breathing session.

10. End in gratitude for the answers and awareness.

Question and Answer: Sensory Expression

At the deep processing level of breaking through sabotages, sensing your emotions and passions enhances the experience of the centering and breathing techniques, increasing the likelihood of realizing the creation.

Emotions open up parts of the mind and heart that are hidden, unless feelings are part of the experience. Experiment with these techniques using deep positive emotions and enjoy watching the results unfold.

1. Do one of the basic centering techniques.

2. Clear the mind. Clear the heart. Clear the Lower Dan Tian (just below the navel).

3. Breathe in. Breathe out.

4. Ask the question. Add feelings, colors, smells and sounds.

5. Breathe in. Pause.

6. Allow for the answer through your feelings, colors, smells and sounds.

7. Breathe out.

8. Continue for several minutes.

Question and Answer: Knowingness

The answers are already available as the questions arise. You may not know the answer, but somewhere the answer exists. This is a great technique for increasing trust and spirituality. Some people want answers and resolution immediately, when actually, impatience may be the core issue.

Rose Rael, one of the author's teachers, said that the secret to creation and solutions is in the knowing. She would send out a request and/or question with her intent while in deep meditation. Often, within 24 hours or a few days, the question would be answered or the desire fulfilled. She had complete trust and faith.

Technique:

1. Do one of the basic centering techniques.

2. Clear the mind. Clear the heart. Clear the Lower Dan Tian (just below the navel).

3. Breathe in. Breathe out.

4. Ask the question. Be clearer, clean up the question to be very concise. Clarity is power.

5. Breathe in. Pause.

6. Allow for the answer in the knowingness of your being.

7. Breathe out. Pause.

8. Repeat. Until an answer comes.

9. When an answer is experienced - expand upon the answer in your heart and mind. *Expansion means to dwell on the answer and enlarge. Mentally, that means to develop the idea in detail, make connections and allow understandings to be made. Emotionally, to feel openly and let those feelings be acknowledged. Spiritually, that means connecting to wisdom and possibly understanding the big picture. For sensory aspects, it may mean body sensations and visuals that bring understanding and insights.*

10. Breathe in. Pause.

11. Experience the result of the information. This is the fruit. *(If you experience no answers or fruit of the experience, then relax and approach it again with trust and intention that an answer will come soon.)*

12. Breathe out. Pause.

13. Repeat for several minutes.

Always be *open* to the possibilities of answers. Keep an open and humble heart, as well as a mind open to possibilities. What may seem the correct path or answer to your logical mind and to others, may actually prove otherwise. Wait upon the universe or God to give an answer spontaneously. Reach deep into the well of knowingness and partake from the spring of universal knowledge. *If you prefer a calmer more centered life, the waiting is worth the fruit of knowingness.*

Clarity of Focus Centering

As your centering becomes more clear and complete and you have experimented with the techniques by enhancing positive emotions, try the opposite technique - clarity of focus. Experiencing clarity of focus includes asking questions, and desiring understanding, while diminishing the mental and emotional fields and opening up the spiritual field.

The blueprint of life is in the spiritual field, and tapping into that field requires the downplaying of mental justification and reasoning, as well as the emotional sensory experience. This centering requires a still mind. The use of mantras and mudras are recommended, but not required. Yoga training is effective at teaching this level.

Reach deep into the well of knowingness, and partake from the spring of universal knowledge.

CHAPTER FOUR

Centering for Joy

Being centered brings a sense of joy in life, while allowing you to remain grounded and present. Using tools such as colors, the energy from your hands, affirmations and mantras, meditations and laughter, bring elements of satisfaction and abundance to our lives.

Rainbow Colors Centering

The rainbow color technique is powerful for visual, sensory-enhanced individuals and is a powerful way to enhance your visual capability. In addition, you can enjoy the power of color in your quest for inner integration, peace and centering.

The rainbow colors centering technique follows the colors of the chakras. These are energy centers around the body. They are discussed in Eastern and yogic disciplines. These spinning wheels of energy extend out from the body for several inches, and sometimes much further. This technique allows you to access and move some of this energy in a beautiful and powerful manner.

When doing the rainbow centering technique, pause after breathing in, and pause after breathing out. This enhances the depth of the creation.

1. Do one of the basic centering techniques.

2. *Experience the colors of the rainbow. Start with the color of* **MAGENTA.**

3. Breathe in.

4. *Visualize the color magenta as an orb large enough for you to enter. Experience the abounding energy and dignity of magenta.*

5. Breathe out.

6. While taking several in and out breaths…

7. *Experience magenta as the calmer, the bridge, and peace.*

8. *Visualize* **RED** *as energy coming up from the ground and centering on the lower hips.*

9. Breathe in.

10. *Experience red as vitality, counteracting fatigue, providing energy, strength and a life-giving force.*

11. Breathe out.

12. While taking several in and out breaths…

13. *Experience red as life instinct, passion and physical strength.*

14. *Visualize* **ORANGE** *as energy flowing from the hips through the lower abdomen.*

15. Breathe in.

16. *Experience orange as letting go of the past, releasing guilt, being cheerful, assimilating life and creating self-empowerment.*

17. Breathe out.

18. While taking several in and out breaths...

19. *Experience orange as emotional freedom, self-esteem and creation.*

20. *Visualize **YELLOW** as rising from the navel and flowing to the bottom of the rib cage.*

21. Breathe in.

22. *Experience yellow as mental power, personal honor, taking care of the self, assimilating life energy and changing fear to trust.*

23. Breathe out.

24. *While taking several in and out breaths...*

25. *Experience yellow as hope, satisfaction and peace.*

26. *Visualize **GREEN** as rising from the rib cage, flowing fully through the chest.*

27. Breathe in.

28. *Experience green as stability, healing, compassion, turning grief to hope, anger to forgiveness, honor to others and love to self.*

29. Breathe out.

30. While taking several in and out breaths...

31. *Experience green as love, wholeness and balance.*

32. *Visualize **TURQUOISE/CYAN** as rising from the upper chest and flowing to the lower part of the throat.*

33. Breathe in.

34. *Experience turquoise as soothing, centering, positive thoughts, supportive, stimulating and refreshing.*

35. Breathe out.

36. While taking several in and out breaths…

37. *Experience turquoise as clarity between emotion and thought, mind and body.*

38. *Visualize **BLUE** as rising from the throat and up to the eyes.*

39. Breathe in.

40. *Experience blue as expressing and following your dream, gregarious communication, positive willpower and energy for body functions.*

41. Breathe out.

42. While taking several in and out breaths…

43. *Experience blue as joy, expression and bonding.*

44. *Visualize **INDIGO** as flowing from the eyes to the forehead.*

45. Breathe in.

46. *Experience indigo as clarity, insight and an inner search for inner peace.*

47. Breathe out.

48. While taking several in and out breaths…

49. *Experience Indigo as intuition and understanding.*

50. *Visualize **VIOLET** as flowing from the forehead to the crown.*

51. Breathe in.

52. *Experience violet as blending emotions and intelligence, relaxing, self-respecting, peaceful, truthful and trusting.*

53. Breathe out.

54. While taking several in and out breaths…

55. *Experience violet as insight and faith.*

56. *Visualize* **WHITE** *as rising from the crown to high above the head.*

57. Breathe in.

58. *Experience white as peace, values, courage, a view of the larger picture of life for all, faith and spiritual devotion.*

59. Breathe out.

60. While taking several in and out breaths…

61. *Experience white as spiritual awareness and divine trust.*

62. *Experience the* **rainbow** *flowing through your being. Dance with the energy. Let the energy dance with you.*

63. Breathe in. Pause.

64. Breathe out. Pause.

65. Experience as much as desired.

It is recommended to start with magenta because it is the melding of colors, the color that reaches down below red and rises to reach violet, from the first chakra to the seventh, encompassing the spine. The other color similar in purpose to magenta is white, as white contains the entire color spectrum. Each of the seven charkas has an associated color and this technique uses both the chakra color and location, so it is a particularly powerful technique.

Hands-On Energy Centering

You and every human have billions of chemical and electrical transactions and events happening every second. Each of these produces and receives energy as a result. This energy is channeled through the body ingeniously. This energy becomes a part of the powerful natural life energy that flows in each person. If you want to use some of this magnificent energy for good, try the hands-on energy centering technique.

This technique can be used to help move pain, reduce pain, focus the centering on a specific area of the body and give comfort. It can be useful when there is stuck energy in the body.

Tracy, a seventeen-year-old, protected her friend from harm by engaging in a fight. She was hit with a powerful punch in the jaw. Tracy's jaw was in pain for a year with no relief. Trying this procedure with the emotional centering technique, she dealt with the associated emotions, while energizing her jaw with some hands-on centering. Tracy moved her jaw in different positions and energized the jaw in those positions. After some focused work, she was amazed how quickly she was able to move her jaw freely.

Technique:

1. Start with a simple centering breath technique.

2. Put your hands on the area of the body that you want to focus the energy into.

3. Direct the focus to that area while doing the centering breath.

4. Leave your hands in that area for at least three minutes.

5. Put your hands around the desired areas in 2 to 3 positions.

6. Leave your hands there for 2 to 3 minutes for each position.

7. (Optional: tighten the muscle after the in-breath and loosen on the out-breath).

For example, if you want to energize the jaw due to soreness or pain, start with the palms on both sides of the jaw. Visualize a green or blue light between your jaw muscles (the masseter and buccinator muscles). Focus your thoughts on the jaw and direct the soreness to go down to the feet and exit the body. Leave the hands there for three minutes. Be sure to take deep, calm breaths, bringing oxygen to the area and clearing out the toxins.

Continue by moving the hands over the TMJ (temporomandibular joint). The palms are held over the area that would be the sideburns for a male. Leave the hands there for three minutes. The TMJ is associated with dental problems, mercury, dehydration and emotions of fear, anger and not speaking out. It helps to visualize the mouth and jaw releasing the pain and problems associated with the pain. Now, you can continue with this procedure going to the neck and shoulders if desired.

Suggestions:

o This energy and centering technique can be done on yourself or on others.

o Experience the energy in colors, feelings and vibrations. Sense the multi-dimensions of the area that is being energized.

o Allow understandings to come to your heart and mind about any blockages. Calmly move them through the body.

o Sometimes if the area receiving the energy grows too hot, it might be better to put your hands around the area rather than directly on it. If the area is too cold, place your hands directly on the area for three minutes, on the areas around the coldness and possibly do hands-on energy on the bottom of the feet. In addition, cold hands or feet are an indication to drink warm or room temperature water.

o   Sometimes the hands-on energy technique will cause some dehydration. To assist in hydrating the body, place your hands on the lower back over the kidney area. Energize this area for three minutes. The kidneys are responsible for water usage and distribution. Also, trace mineral supplementation may be helpful.

Affirmations and Mantras

Create an affirmation or mantra that is in alignment with the desires of your heart and in alignment with the universe (God's will). The value of an affirmation is dependent upon you. If you are in alignment and centered, the affirmation is powerful. If you are trying to convince yourself of the validity of the affirmation, then the creation and permanency of it is unstable and unlikely.

Surrender the inner, negative self-talk and replace it with *positive expectancy*. Negative self-talk will fight your efforts with affirmations. If there is emotional resistance, consider the section on Emotional centering.

Often, individuals use affirmations to escape pain and suffering. They are trying to manipulate their life and/or the lives of others. If affirmations are used in this manner, there might be negative long-term results, or the results will probably not come as expected.

John wanted to save his company. He was willing to do anything except face the facts. He decided if he just had enough money everything *would work out. He put together an affirmation of "I will have $125,000 by Tuesday." He posted the affirmations everywhere and requested all employees of his small company to say the affirmation several times a day. The affirmation worked. The money came in, but it came from selling equipment rather than new work. His company did not survive. The affirmation needed to be clearer and specific about how the money would come and more importantly, John needed to process his emotional and mental issues causing his company problems.*

Shauna wanted her business to expand fast. Affirmations just were not working. She decided to do deep centering work and process through some emotions and beliefs that were blocking her success. After doing her part, the affirmations were very successful. She was amazed how quickly the creation came with the affirmations when she became centered.

Use some of the following examples and adjust them to your wants and desires:

o   *I joyously receive the light and love of God. I accept his abundance and peace in all areas of my life.*

o   *I can be wealthy and fulfill my passion and honor my values.*

o   *I am worthy of God's love.*

o   *I am loving and am worthy to receive love.*

o   *I am full of vigor and life.*

o   *I create joy in all areas of my life.*

o   *I think, feel and act in balance and unity with my true, whole self.*

o   *I enjoy my relationships. My relationships support me.*

o *I create a body full of life and let go of all unnecessary baggage, weight and burden.*

o *I create supportive and abundant relationships.*

o *I choose to experience life with fullness of expression and joy.*

o *I am the worthy recipient of God's abundance, joy, gifts, peace, light and love.*

o *I enjoy all situations of life.*

o *I allow and ask the universe and God and angels to support me.*

o *I am grateful for the abundant support of God and the universe.*

o *My body is safe to be its optimal weight and size.*

o *My body enjoys being its optimal weight and size.*

o *I am worthy and deserve my hopes, intents and dreams.*

Use one of these affirmation examples, or another of your choosing. Let the energy of the affirmation flow into every pore and every cell of your body. Gradually do this with each breath in. Exhale any obstacle to the affirmation. Feel appreciation for the strength and growth that it gives you.

Start with the heart centering technique discussed earlier, in combination with the affirmation method. Gradually move the focus to the brain and integrate the two sides of the brain with the affirmation: "My Brain communicates freely and openly, always expanding and safely integrating life, learning, understanding and wisdom."

Advanced: Use this technique with the Nostril Breath Centering technique. And use the senses, passion and emotion to enhance and deepen the experience.

Blockage Removal Centering

During one of the centering techniques, if there is a sensation of a blockage, identify the blockage. See if you can imagine it as a shape or form, and color it. You may try to communicate with the blockage and sense why it is there. Ask direct questions to help move the energy or pain through the body, such as, "What is your intent?" or "What do you want to do or become?"

By addressing the blockage, you can discover its purpose and release it, restoring flow in the body and mind, and gaining new understanding. In other words, the blockages are great teachers, teaching you about yourself, showing you some of the subconscious sabotages imbedded deep within your being.

Pain Release

Centering is one of the most powerful ways to deal with pain. Centering helps a person who is scattered, focusing on pain and other problems, to come back home to self. If you are scattered, fearful or angry, you are not centered. If you are not grounded, or you are so stuck in the mud of your life that you cannot see past your nose, let alone seek divine help, you are not centered. Centering is only possible when you live in the moment. The centering techniques will enable you to come back to self, and live in the moment.

NOTE: *There is no pain in the moment. None. Some ask how can that be? Try it. There is no pain when the self is integrated, aligned, centered and focused in a single moment, present in time; neither in the past nor in the future.*

Pain release centering is a wonderful tool to use for both physical and emotional pain. There are two options. The first includes guided imagery. The second uses the energy from your hands.

Pain Release with Visualization for Seeking Understanding

1. Find a pain or stress in your body. Visualize and focus on that pain or stress.

2. Imagine what that pain looks like, feels like or other sensory attributes.

3. Breathe

4. Imagine the shape and form out in front of you.

5. Give it a mouth and let it speak to you.

6. While directing your focus at the form that came from the pain, ask what its purpose is for you, or "why are you here"?

7. Sometimes the information can provide insight. Seek for an answer that will reveal to you what emotional conflict you don't want to face in the present or an emotional pain of the near past.

8. Do an emotional centering process as mentioned in this publication.

9. Choose to release the negative beliefs emotions. The pain is just an alarm of what you are suppressing.

10. Once you have learned or embraced the understanding of the pain, let it go. Send it to the earth, the sun or the angels to be changed and transformed.

11. If there is some pain remaining, repeat the process.

12. When the process is complete, take a deep cleansing breath, and drink water. You may want to take some magnesium and vitamin C.

Use the water meditation centering technique if the pain continues. Of course, if the pain persists, see a professional for assistance. Your meditation will make any professional help much more effective.

Pain Release Using Touch and Breathing

1. Use your hands and touch the area of pain.

2. Leave your hands there for 3 minutes.

3. While the hands are there, begin the centering technique of breathing deeply and focusing on the pain area.

4. After three minutes, move your hands to a position closer to your feet and leave them there for one minute.

5. While the hands are in the new position, breathe and center deeply focusing on the new area.

6. After one minute, move your hands to the next position closer to your feet and leave them there for one minute.

7. While the hands are in the new position, breathe and center deeply focusing on the new area.

8. Keep this up until the hands are on the feet and complete the process at the feet.

9. Complete with one minute of deeply cleansing the body with imagery and breath.

Using breathing techniques while experiencing pain will create an accelerated path for the brain to start healing the body. Often, with major pain, the brain is so busy dealing with the pain indicators that the healing energy is diverted to the symptoms rather than the cause of the problem.

Clarity vs. Confusion

Confusion can easily creep upon us like a mist of a morning fog if we have too much busy-ness going on. Not getting enough sleep, eating a bit too much sugar, trying to do too much, or extending ourselves past our capacity can bring an element of confusion to our minds. In the brain, we have a system to deal with confusion. The neurotransmitter, acetylcholine, is used throughout the body and in the brain and helps you pay attention and keep a clear mind. When a person is confused, this chemical is in high demand.

Most likely, there are several parts of the brain competing for attention, and you might have conflicting ideas of what to do next, what you should have done, or how to "sort it all out."

Clarity is an organized state of mind, not requiring a great deal of energy. On the other hand, confusion is a lot of work. Yet, most people spin their lives in confusion the majority of the time. I find it interesting that most people want to "figure it out" before they can let an issue rest. The truth is, that is not the path to success and peace. It is when you are clear and calm that your mind is open so that you can see the correct path to take.

Confusion is similar to tossing thoughts, like darts, into a fog. We may go into a state of panic, throwing those thought-darts at any sound, light, or motion, with the hope that they might reach the correct target, yet not knowing whether they did or not. This only increases our confusion.

In applying mindfulness to our state of confusion, we may begin by focusing on gratitude, and appreciation for what we have been given. Confusion can be seen simply as a puzzle. From the place of gratitude, we can appreciate the value of the puzzles in our lives. A puzzle is a gift, because without any puzzles we would have nowhere to go, nothing to learn, and zero possibilities. Be grateful for the opportunity to solve each puzzle.

Next, notice your conflicts, are any of them based in "**fear**"? If so, the confusion is not about truth, it is about safety of self or others. For instance, our need for approval is a safety issue. Are your conflicts about "**anger**"? If so, they about unfulfilled expectations. Our expectations and the Stories and filters we create around them create a fantasy. Unfulfilled fantasy expectations create conflicts that are never based on truth.

Clarity is the opposite of clutter. Excess thought and excess emotion lead to a cluttered life. When you are manifesting clutter, you are attempting to hold onto more than you have space for. No one has the capacity to hold onto everything. Even God creates a good wind storm every once in a while, to clear out the air.

Clarity is about truth, not emotion. Emotion can color your day or smother your life. It is your choice.

Restoring Clarity

Do the following breathing technique with the intention of clearing the fog and clearing the mind. Be sure to read the sections about conflict and aligning your mind and heart. Then, notice how this technique of breathing facilitates clarity.

Take a deep, cleansing breath.

1. Hold the Nourish Earth & Lungs* Mode. (See the Clarity to Release Position, from the following Hand Positions for Restoring Clarity chart.)

2. Slowly inhale and exhale with a long, deep breath.

3. Focus on the position of your hands.

4. Breathe several long and slow breaths.

5. Extend your attention beyond the area of your hands, to your head.

6. Extend your attention to your body.

7. Extend your attention to the room.

8. Extend your attention beyond the room and into a calm, serene nature scene.

9. Imagine you are breathing with the clouds.

10. Release your attention and let go of conscious thought.

11. Nothing else matters now. Only the breath.

12. After many moments or many minutes, come back to your body and the hands touching your face.

13. Notice your mind. Notice your feelings. Notice your body.

14. If your mind feels calm and clear, enjoy this moment.

15. Repeat, as needed.

Note: If your mind is still racing, go through the cycle again WITHOUT any of the inner chatter of "needs" or "have-tos."

Hand Modes/Positions for Restoring Clarity	
*Nourish & Connect Mode	Two hands, respective fingertips touching (index to index tips, etc.) Palms slightly apart
Clarity to Release Confusion	Using the Nourish & Connect mode, place the thumbs at the point of your chin and the index fingers between the brows, at the 3rd eye.
Thymus Calming Mode	Using one hand with all fingertips touching, point and touch the chest 4 finger widths below the sternal notch.

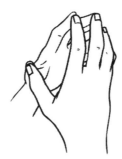

Nourish & Connect Mode*

Hold the hands facing each other, with the palms 1″ apart. With the fingers spread apart ¼″, touch each fingertip to their corresponding fingertip on the other hand. Thus, thumb tip to thumb tip, index to index tip, middle to middle tip, ring to ring tip, little finger to little fingertip.

Compassion Meditation with Clarity Breath

Do the Clarity breath

1. While breathing and centering with your breath, notice any negative thoughts that arise.

2. Visualize an individual that you may have sent a negative thought toward.

3. See that the person has a covering of negativity, and imagine unzipping that negativity.

4. Discard the negative energy.

5. See the light that is in all people, beyond any of us, but in all of us.

6. Visualize sending compassion and the light of the universe flowing to them.

7. Hold compassion for yourself, and allow a river of soft light to flow through you.

8. Be grateful for the divine and universal love & light that is supporting you and all of us.

Joy Meditation

You may be involved in healing modalities to take away pain, rid yourself of problems and avoid the undesirable aspects of your life. However, true change really happens when you take responsibility. One of those responsibilities is to choose gratitude and joy. Many people focus on doubt, fear and pain, thus reaping storms of life with stress and confusion. By choosing joy and gratitude, you can transform, reduce the number of storms in your life and bring ease in times of conflict. By choosing joy, you are creating a foundation for what you want. Spontaneous creation is the fruit of the seeds of joy.

There are three joy meditations. The first two are focused on the physical parts of the brain that has been shown to trigger joy in individuals. Consider the literature over the past few years of brain surgeries that have caused spontaneous reactions and memories in patients, independent of the patient's experience lying on the table; spontaneous memories, terror, euphoria and joy have been reported.

You do not have to have an error in brain surgery to experience some of these memories. Use this centering technique that will bring joy easily.

1. Relax, take a deep breath and slowly exhale.

2. Visualize and imagine your focus going to the space between the eyebrows.

3. Imagine going into the lower center of the brain, one and one half inches behind the eyes and centered from left to right. This region is part of the Limbic brain. It includes the Septal area of the brain just in front of the hypothalamus gland, the Fornix, the Hippocampus, the Entorhinal Cortex, and the Parahippocampus. When these nuclei of the brain are in synchronization, short term memory is smooth, emotions do not get overwhelming, and long term memory is easily accessed. More importantly for this meditation, focus on this area with the intent of releasing suppressed anger and frustration, and inviting in joy. Visualize the feeling of joy flowing easily through these brain nuclei.

4. Start with a focus on the limbic areas of the brain.

5. Breathe in, with intent to send energy into this limbic area.

6. Pause to let the energy flow freely.

7. Breathe out excess concern, blockage, etc.

8. Pause.

9. Breathe in with intent, to send fresh energy into the limbic area.

10. Continue as long as desired. Enliven this area of the brain and enjoy the euphoria.

11. As the joy grows, expand it into the entire body.

Another area to focus on, is the connection between the Pineal gland (the melatonin gland) and the Intralaminar nucleus of the Thalamus (the switchboard operator region of the brain). The Intralaminar area of the Thalamus relays pain information and possibly personal and spiritual awareness of self and the soul.

Use the above procedure for the Limbic brain nuclei, and add imagery of the pineal gland, thalamus gland (it is in the center of the brain) and the neurotransmitters - serotonin, melatonin. Focus and open up your mind for a calm peaceful journey of joy.

Suggestions of Other Brain Positions:

Hypothalamus: (lower center): Regulates Hormones, Communication Central, Circadian Rhythms, Body Temperature, Digestion, Calm, Peace, Clarity, Strength in the midst of the storm and Forgiveness.

Thalamus: (just above the hypothalamus): Calm, Peace, Euphoria, Clarity and Sensory Integration.

Frontal Lobes: Heightened Awareness, Cognition, Clarity of Analysis and Trust.

Amygdala: (right behind the frontal lobes): Release of Rage, Release of Terror, Release of Fear - Replace with Courage, Peace, Social and Emotional Integration.

Brain Stem: Release Terror, Release Fear – Replace with Trust, Safety, Balance, Love, Hope and Faith.

Cerebellum: (base of skull): Replace Struggle, Fear, Confusion, and being out of synchronization, with Comfort, Warmth, Safety, Serendipity and Joy.

Gratitude and Joy Centering

This Gratitude and Joy centering is based on feelings and visualizations. It is combined with the energy emitted by the emotions of gratitude, joy, peace, euphoria and other positive power intents.

1. Relax, take a deep breath and slowly exhale.

2. Focus on the upper abdomen.

3. Breathe in with the intent of *satisfaction.* That satisfaction is flowing to this area of your body.

4. Pause, allowing the energy to flow freely.

5. Breathe out excess anxiety, tightness, worry and mistrust.

6. Pause.

7. Breathe in *gratitude* for your breath.

8. Breathe out all negative judgments, especially judgments that have led to resentments. Breathing out resentments releases links to your burdens.

9. Breathe in *gratitude* for the senses – taste, touch, feel, see, hear, smell, movement, gustatory and intuition.

10. Breathe out any negative thoughts.

11. Breathe in *gratitude* for the simple things of life.

12. Breathe out any negative feelings.

13. Breathe in *gratitude* for hope and how it feels in your soul.

14. Breathe out pain that others have caused you.

15. Breathe in understanding and appreciation for the wisdom developed from those painful experiences.

(Be creative – introduce your gratitude from your heart and soul) Continue with the gratitude cycle and then go to joy, peace, euphoria and other positive power intents.

This technique can be combined with the Joy Meditation. The time to do the gratitude centering technique is not only when you want to feel good, like a cup of hot tea and a warm hug, but also when life has given you a couple of bumps that hurt. Gratitude brings back reality, resets, re-calibrates and helps restart your life without the pain of blame, criticism and resentment.

God gives us the abundance of life. We are such a blessed people. Compare your life to the lives of those who lived just two hundred years ago. The luxury that you now enjoy is greater than that of kings and queens of past eras. Be grateful that when you are able to express this understanding, you can see past the fog of daily life, and live a life beyond the confines of suppressing boundaries.

Your state of mind and heart determines your life experience. Thank God daily for that awareness.

Soaring Meditation

Meditations enhance our possibilities and improve on how we interact with life. Use this technique with any of the breathing and centering techniques - preferably with soft music.

Be the bird of freedom
Soaring
Floating on the waves of air
Feeling
Sensing the moisture of a cloud
Seeing
Gasping at the vastness of the forest
Smelling
Grasping the crispness of the fragrance

Experiencing
Fulfilling all the senses in a moment
Loving
Feeling God basking in creation
Thrilling
Swimming straight through the air
Accelerating
Flying toward creation
Assimilating
Sweeping it deep into the soul
Changing
Soaring up high for fruition
Releasing
Satisfying the inner soul
Breathing
Calming in gratitude, free, full
Living

Nature Meditation

Integrate the mind and heart, with nature meditations. Use this and other similar meditations to bring yourself back into focus and peace.

Calm yourself in the field of nature
Notice the trees, foliage and flowers
The hills, mountains, clouds, sky

Pause with the sky, see the blue
Notice the sun, the rays abundant
Feel the radiance enter the top of your head

Let father sky enlighten your soul
Let the mind open channels
Bringing clarity and hope

Let the warmth flow deep within
From the head, neck, shoulders
Chest, arms, abdomen, legs

Feel the light in the brain and heart
Let the pulse of life resonate
Between the two as one silently

Send the light through the body
Focus on the feet, toes and further
Deep communion with the earth

Receive from the earth warmth
Minerals, grounding, peace
Quiet, balance, strength

Nourish your feet, knees and legs
Savor the deep love up in the intestines
Food from mother earth in the stomach

Let mother earth and father sky
Meld their two energies consisting of
Light, love, nourishment and strength

Be in oneness, feel wholeness
Feel stillness, Feel
Be

Return to Nature, Return to Joy.

CHAPTER FIVE

Centered Health and Emotions

For those more technically minded, here is an additional note about the connection between the brain, body and emotions:

In the brain, the hypothalamus produces neuro-peptides. These neuro-peptides are protein based and have specific functions.

Candace Pert identified neuro-peptides that were associated with fear, anger, frustration, happiness, joy, and other emotions. When individuals dwelt on those emotions, the hypothalamus would send these neuro-peptides to the cells of the body. When a neuro-peptide docked with a receptor site of a cell, the cell was physically modified by the neuro-peptide.

Remember some neuro-peptides are emotionally based. Thus, changing your emotions and your thinking can indeed change your physical reality. Of course, an emotional state, positive or negative, can be modified with more clarity and congruency with the centering techniques.

In fact, according to Dr. Pert, "the radical discovery we made was that every neuropeptide receptor we could find in the brain is also on the surface of the human monocyte. Immune cells also make, store, and secrete the neuropeptides themselves. In other words, the immune cells are making the same chemicals that we conceive of as controlling mood in the brain." (Candace Pert, PhD.)

Personal empowerment is at your fingertips. Your entire body is a factory for both physical and emotional changes. By creating congruency and clarity through centering techniques, can you can initiate positive changes today, throughout your entire body.

Emotional Centering

Do not ignore emotionally upsetting problems and stress. If you use these techniques to rid yourself of pain and to find your center, but you attempt to ignore emotional upsets and mental strain, you will not find the peace you are looking for. Emotional centering is key to the complete centering process.

Often emotional processing is only performed from the mind. This is mental justification and rationalization. True emotional healing requires going deep into the heart and the body to allow for emotional cleansing. Start cleaning and clearing the emotions by speaking them out with feeling, drawing them out, writing them out, walking or stretching them out, and of course, breathing them out.

Deep-seated fear and repressed anger will start to leave if you give them a door and a pathway. Often the pain is so intense that the body thinks it is better to leave it inside. Over time, a soul in pain will render a life filled with pain. Be patient and trust the breathing techniques and start expressing the old emotions in a safe place with someone you trust or to yourself.

The next part of emotional centering consists of seeing those times in your life when you have felt fear and anger. Express those feelings for those times. Compare the events and see the patterns. Most often there are patterns and similar directions you have taken because of your pain. Notice that these directions have led you to your current state, along with certain beliefs, particular relationships and situations.

Notice the blame you put upon others or yourself. Blame is better stated: Be-Lame. Over time, blame destroys your spiritual and emotion maturity. Once you are able to identify the patterns and see that the beliefs you hang onto seem to be more important than your joy and peace, then you can start to make new decisions. Choose to be happy instead of having to "be right" about what others did to you. Yes, there are many that betray, but you might have harmed someone yourself at one time or another. The energy that it takes to hold and keep resentments makes people sick and entraps them in pain.

So, the next step is to actually see the value of the pain that caused you emotional grief. Every event can be of value to you. Every experience is growth. Experience the benefit, let go of the judgment and release yourself from the prison of negative emotions.

Use one of the centering breath techniques to bring focus to your process.

1. Express your emotions with feeling from the body and heart.

2. Recall similar emotions and time frames.

3. Express emotions from those experiences.

4. Mentally consider similarities, patterns, beliefs, etc.

5. Let go of the blame to yourself or others in these experiences.

6. See how you have compensated and acknowledge any payoffs.

7. Learn from these experiences and understand how to grow from them.

8. Feel gratitude in heart and mind for the experiences and wisdom.

This technique will assist you in centering emotionally. If you are having trouble letting go of the blame and the pain, then consider seeking professional help. Remember to do deep, centering breath work with your emotional processing. It allows the cells to release and move the energies that you do not have cognitive understanding or awareness of. Most real, emotional centering is completed by the subconscious, if you trust the process.

Centered Health and Healing

Your body is full of alarms. When an alarm needs to be activated, your body reacts with a variety of responses. Some of the body reactions are physical, muscle responses, such as spasms, aches, tightness, pain, or weakness. Some of the body reactions are emotional feelings of anger, fear, upset, sadness, or tears.

Some of the body reactions are gastro-intestinal i.e. nausea, pain, gas, indigestion, diarrhea, or constipation. Some reactions are headaches, backaches, dry tongue, or a twitch in an eye. The list could go on and on.

These are what I call biological-fire alarms. The body is trying to get a message across but it does not speak your native language of English, Spanish, or Japanese. Usually an alarm goes off when there is problem. For example, in the home, there are alarms for fire, theft, heating, water, and cooking, etc. If a fire alarm is triggered, you don't take a hammer and slam the alarm or break it all into pieces. If a fire alarm goes off, you pay attention and take the necessary actions, for safety.

It is the same with the human body. Let the biological-fire alarms inform you, alert you, and assist you in your path of healing, do not let the need for instant pain relief hide the message being sent.

Bio-fire alarms can be identified and labeled. You can identify the associations between the variety of bio-fire alarms. With enough clues, you can find the connections between the physical, emotional, mental, energy, and spiritual areas of your health.

First, you may wish to have a health practitioner such as a chiropractor, a doctor, physical therapist, psychologist, kinesiologist, or other therapist advise you with their insight into what the bio-fire alarm is trying to signify.

While medical attention is often warranted and even recommended, there is one problem. Most practitioners and people do not see depth to those bio-fire alarms. They only see symptoms.

The bio-fire alarms actually are telling a story. The story is deeper than one level of understanding. For example, if there is a muscle spasm of the peroneus muscle located on the lateral side of the calf, it may actually signify a problem with the bladder, the colon, or stomach. It also may signify a problem with the control issues in a person's life, suppressed anger, toxins in the elimination system, or overwhelming demands on a person. It could signify a need to stop performing too many tasks and pleasing people along the way. Any or all these may be what the peroneus muscle is screaming about.

Wisdom then, would be to consult with a medical professional as common sense would dictate, and in addition, address the underlying issues indicated by the "bio-fire alarm".

The term "bio-fire alarms" is the name applied by this author for what most authors and practitioners refer to as body reflex or response areas. For the science behind some of the reasons the body creates these bio-fire alarms, refer to some of the books in the bibliography, specifically: Revolutionary Way of Thinking, by Charles Krebs, Energy Medicine by James Oschman, and Neuro-Acupuncture by Z.H. Cho and E.K. Wong.

In general, as the fetus develops the nervous system of the muscles, they merge with the other nervous systems. The innervations of the nerves to the other systems set up the groundwork for reflexes and for visceral responses to be inter-related with the body and the brain.

We are born with neuro-muscular reflexes, referred to as Primitive Reflexes. Most reflexes are there for warning or for spontaneous survival reactions. For example, the sucking reflex is important because the survival need for the child to eat causes the child to suck on the breast of his/her mother.

In the mother, the sucking of the child on the nipple of the breast causes a message to be sent to "the paraventricular nucleus of the hypothalamus in the brain, which in turn instigates the release of Oxytocin from the posterior pituitary into circulation, leading to the contraction of smooth muscles of mammary tissues, which pumps milk from the breast. This reflex becomes easily conditioned to various behavioral cues from the infant." (J. Pankseep, Affective Neuroscience).

The brain and body of the mother can become so in tune with the child that before the child touches the nipple the mother knows what is coming and her body will start producing the necessary milk unintentionally. This plasticity of the brain, nervous system and the emotional system of the body is phenomenal. The body has so many messages that are stored and transmitted through muscles, nerves, emotions, intuition, etc. Keep an open mind and find out what your body is trying to communicate to you.

Centered Health is the awareness that bio-fire alarms exist, and the willingness to seek clarity of the biological and emotional nature of your body. If you first reach for a pill before seeking for awareness or clarity, then you are not being centered with your health. It is fantastic that there are drugs and herbs for our benefit; yet, if pills lead to denial of hidden messages, the day may come when pills are ineffective.

The best of both worlds is to make sure that your physical and mental needs are taken care of. While in that process, consider the other possibilities of what your body may be speaking to you. Your body speaks a language that is faster and much broader than verbal communication. It communicates a language that only the "seeker" can connect to. By doing in-depth centering techniques, you may begin to hear the hidden messages that are continually being sent to you.

After seeking professional assistance for your health issues, you may want additional input on that process. You may contact an energy kinesiologist, who is trained on the combination and depth of messages of these bio-fire alarms.

Accomplishing Centered Health and Healing requires a desire to bring the body, the mind, and the heart into congruency by seeking answers beyond the obvious. Choosing to process through fears that are keeping you sick, allows you to discover why you are physically held back in life. Those who choose to do this find clarity, health, joy, and increased energy. Remember, once you discover a truth and experience awareness, refrain from over-analyzing.

Do some of the centering techniques to regain clarity and healing in the body, surrender the pain and emotional judgments, then go on with life.

Technique:

For your own personal health centering experience:

1. Choose your favorite centering technique in this book.

2. Identify your physical health problem – the *bio-fire alarm*.

3. Trace the associated mental, emotional, spiritual and other possibilities that may be attached to this problem.

4. Use the emotional and visualization techniques in this book.

5. There is usually a story of negative beliefs and emotions that support the *bio-fire alarm*. Use some of the centering techniques to allow your sub-conscious to bring this story to the surface.

6. The story that keeps the body non-healthy may include events that happened in your life. Or it may be beliefs and emotions that you cherish more than getting yourself healthy. It is usually frustrating memories of events, beliefs, emotions, and judgments to people that create the obstacles to healing. Remember it is not the outside that causes the problem. It is the inside judgment and internal reactions that cause the problem.

7. Choose which is more important: Health or Judgment. (If you hold frustration or judgment to others, to events, or to your own body, then healing is substantially compromised).

8. Employing forgiveness, and asking the universe and God to forgive your enemy is one of the most powerful healing techniques.

9. If forgiveness is not attainable yet, then use the visualization technique and imagine (while doing deep centering breath) that you release toxins and heaviness from your body. Release the pain to the universe and to God.

10. For chronic problems, we advise seeking professional help. Also, for chronic problems, the centering techniques used to create congruency need to include an attitude shift - from blame to gratitude. Commit to continue to use the deep centering techniques daily.

11. Support your body nutritionally, with the appropriate nutrients and lifestyle.

12. Support your body with clear, congruent thoughts and feelings for a great life that will bring joy to you and your loved ones.

(For classes on this and other techniques contact the author at info@livebyheart.net with the word *classes* in the subject line).

Health is a mirror of what is inside your mind and heart. Your words are a mirror of what's inside your heart and physical body. Your feelings are a mirror of what's inside your mind and body.

The following charts are some samples of *bio-fire alarms*. These charts include possible meanings and suggested affirmations. These are only possibilities. These are not meant for medical information. Seek medical advice on your health problems. These are for your enlightenment and centering assistance.

Physiologically Based Bio-Fire Alarms

A sampling of some physiologically based *bio-fire alarms* and possible meanings:

Problem area	Physical Symptoms or Contributors	Emotional Mental Symptoms	Affirmations
Abscesses	Bacteria, infection in glands. TMJ, jaw, axis, atlas, neck, small intestines, colon.	Lonely, longing, hidden secrets, repressed expression.	I open my expressions. I speak the truth and I respect myself.
Adrenals	Driven personality. Hormonal imbalance. Sugar imbalances. Colon issues, Kidneys.	Panic, Fear of stopping. Motivation based on fear or perfectionism. Procrastination.	I am motivated by choice, by joy, by intrigue. I stop, listen and experience the moment. I follow my goals with ease.
Arm	Organs of the upper body. Heart, Gall Bladder, Lungs, Large Intestines.	Fear of grasping and holding what is important. Holding heart emotions of others. Wanting to take care of another. Fear of feeling life fully.	I embrace life and others with a sharing attitude.

Problem area	Physical Symptoms or Contributors	Emotional Mental Symptoms	Affirmations
Arthritis	Toxicity. Mineral Deficiency. Minerals not in proper balance. Immune system overload. Digestive issues, Lymph and colon.	Bitterness, blame, rough feelings. Sadness, jealousy, deep-seated anger. Determination but turned to silent hopelessness.	I am free to feel. I am free to move and express myself. I let go of all the emotional judgments and resentments. I learn from life. All things work for my good.
Asthma	Holding breath, low blood sugar, pH imbalance, adrenal overload, Vit.C, B Complex.	Abandonment, panic due to separation distress, holding on, smothering, afraid to deal with life, burden, grief, longing, rejection.	I release my fears. I am open to flow with life. I open to the next part of my life. God is always there for me. I am safe and secure. I am loved.
Bladder	Greens, high toxicity, digestive issues, colon toxicity, dehydration.	Control, repressed anger, holding on to emotions or beliefs that are toxic to self	I am free. I am safe to let go of the past. I am in control of my body and life. I release my resentments.

Problem area	Physical Symptoms or Contributors	Emotional Mental Symptoms	Affirmations
Blood Pressure (seek advice from health professional)	Constricted veins. Electrolytes, digestive aids. Colon and lymph clearing. Massage of neck downward motion. Cayenne.	Out of Control. Burden and overwhelm. Stubbornness. Feeling of doing it alone and determination.	I relax. I trust God. I love myself. I let go of my judgments and resentments of others. I am open to the perceptions of others. I am clear about my values but I don't worry about the values of others. I am grounded with God and nature.
Cancer (this is not for diagnosis – see your health professional).	Lymph, liver, and colon sluggishness. Major toxicity. (Please see a health care professional.)	Lack of forgiveness. Resentment. Major grief and hatred. Secret pain and judgment.	I love life. I forgive. I let go of all pain and judgment. I really love life and life it fully now. I have fun.
Diabetes	Insulin reactions. Liver, kidney, and spleen sluggishness. Lack of fiber. Lack of exercise. Digestive issues.	Suppressed anger, bitterness, resentment and hate. Sweetness not satisfied. Have to be right.	I flow with life. I enjoy the sweetness of each day and each person. I learn from everyone. I let go of every resentment to every person and event.
Eyes	Digestion of carbohydrates Vitamin C, bioflavonoids, Vitamin A, and glutathione.	Not wanting to see or experience, denial. Hope becoming hopeless. Loss of focus.	I see what is and I learn and grow from life. I enjoy and love what is. I desire, hope, with expectancy not high expectations.

Problem area	Physical Symptoms or Contributors	Emotional Mental Symptoms	Affirmations
Fatigue	Diet problems. Lifestyle is too fast paced, or Emotional issues. Eating too much sugar, wheat, diary, or soda. Candida, colon, lymph toxicity. Mineral deficiency. Fats and Proteins.	Denial. Not wanting to see the past or the future. Carrying burdens of worrying, pleasing. Deep seated emotions of fear, anger, sadness, and frustration.	I can be happy without pleasing everyone. I do not have to be saved to get well. I do not have to save to be happy. God is my support. I am willing to see what is real. I am grateful and happy.
Fibromyalgia	Candida overgrowth, yeast, colon toxicity, lymph toxicity, mineral deficiency, green foods, digestion.	Emotional overload, not listening to body signals and not listening to their intuition. Lack of forgiveness with the appearance of forgiveness. Stubborn.	I choose to take care of me. I choose to listen to my inner guides and divine influence. I choose to be truthful and to let go of any resentment.
Gall Bladder	Indigestion of fats and some proteins.	Indecision, Resentments, Regrets, Stubborn, not willing to move forward.	I love myself. I forgive others. I clear the clutter and choose. I act and experience life.

Problem area	Physical Symptoms or Contributors	Emotional Mental Symptoms	Affirmations
Headaches	Indigestion, bio-chemical issues, hormonal fluctuations, adrenal stresses, blood sugar stresses, liver.	Anger, excessive analyzing, emotional upheavals, fear of dealing with reality, holding onto the past.	I trust life with all its possibilities. I focus on creating congruency and abundance.
Headache Front	Sinus, gastric and small intestinal inflammations.	Worry, overly concerned, self-pity, self-blame, intense anger suppressed, sadness.	I love and respect myself and others. Life is an opportunity.
Headache Back	Carbohydrate indigestion, lymphatic stress.	Suppressed anger, excessive pleasing, fear of seeing, fear of connecting, wanting to escape.	I spontaneously live in all areas of live. I am richly connected with the universe.
Headache Top	Candida overgrowth, back or nerve problems, lymphatic sluggishness.	Suppressed emotions of all types. Anger to someone close, Fear of moving forward, trepidation. Learning overwhelming.	I am open to receive God's love and wisdom.

Problem area	Physical Symptoms or Contributors	Emotional Mental Symptoms	Affirmations
Heart Problems	Colon & digestive problems. Too many fats and proteins that are not digested or assimilated. Physically not integrated. Suppression.	Holding on to grief. Money and relationship issues. Carrying others burdens. Suppression of feelings.	I let go of grief. I trust my loved ones will be fine. I love life today and let go of inner pain.
Hip	Calcium, Magnesium, Hormonal, Colon, Dehydration, TMJ, Toxicity issues.	Relationship issues, Carrying the burdens of others, Money Issues, Boundary issues.	I am safe & grounded. I don't need others to save or make me safe. I choose to enjoy my life with my relationships. I balance my finances and relationships.
Hypoglycemia	Sugar and insulin reactions. Lack of fiber. Lack of exercise. Too many sugars & carbs. Protein indigestion. Colon and pancreas.	Lack of trust. Life is full of surprises. Pleasing others above the self. Belief that God will only help if you perform perfectly.	Life is full of fun. I welcome the adventure. I trust God to bless me. I allow God and the universe to assist me. I feel my heart. I am courage.

Problem area	Physical Symptoms or Contributors	Emotional Mental Symptoms	Affirmations
Immune Issues	Inflammation. Lacking trace minerals and macro minerals. Excess drugs, antibiotics, herbs. Over eating or over-indulging in other addictions. Lack of greens and digestible fats and proteins.	Lack of safety. Lack of freedom. Lack of identity. Fear of being attacked. Never fully resting. Either on edge or overwhelmed past anxiety. Suppressed anxiety, fear, rage. Root and Sacral Plexus issues.	I pace myself. I am an opportunity for growth and adventure. I am safe and free today. I am divine and I am having a human experience. I create friends and family that honor and respect me. I listen and connect to others with understanding.
Jaw, TMJ issues	Cranial pressure, Eustachian tube infection, lymph and glandular infections. Protein indigestion.	Terror or trauma stuck. Inability to speak the truth. Lack of courage. Lack of integrity with goals and aspirations. Rage.	I speak the truth and listen to my inspiration. I am free of rage and anger. I am courage. I am complete with God Determination is second nature to me.
Kidneys	Dehydration. Colon problems.	Fear, Dread, Panic. Standing alone. Lack of trust. Blocking the Chi of life.	I open to universal chi. I assimilate water. I let go of the toxins of life. I am faith and trust.

Problem area	Physical Symptoms or Contributors	Emotional Mental Symptoms	Affirmations
Knee	Colon, Bladder, Lymph, adrenal, glandular issues.	Betrayal, Stuck, Mind and Heart going in two different directions, anger.	I let go of the past and look forward with enthusiasm. I am safe in relationships. I create and walk on the path of a great future.
Large Intestines	Excess sugar and wheat, lack of fiber. Sedentary lifestyle.	Holding onto the past. Withholding from life. Blame, Hate. Past garbage clouds current possibility.	I gladly let go of the past and make room for beneficial change. I learn from the past. I am clear. I am for insight.
Liver	Excess Stress, Junk Food, Excess Sugar, Excess Protein.	Anger, Bitterness, Excess sadness, Excess emotion, Controlling.	I trust. I lead with God as my guide. I release all negative emotions and regrets and frustrations.
Lungs	Breathing shallow, immune system compromised.	Grief, panic, shame, loneliness, hopeless, confusion.	I desire. I expand into life. I breathe in the gifts of God now. I am alive and share.

Problem area	Physical Symptoms or Contributors	Emotional Mental Symptoms	Affirmations
Manic (consult your health care practitioner).	Cells of the body are starved for certain vitamins, minerals and other nutrients. Fatty acids and "carb" indigestion. In need of safe and grounded energy.	Out of control, so the mind speeds up to compensate or to deny. Fear of the future based upon the past. Fear and flawed intuition due to health, abuse, and dirty energy fields. Unrealistic.	I breathe in new life and let go of old fears, angers, and abuse. I am safe now. I love what is right now. I relax and visualize my body grounding to earth, nature and wellbeing. I am real.
Memory	Oxygen, Glucose, Toxicity, Candida, Sugar, Gluten, Digestion, Colon issues. Lack of focus and trauma. Fatty acids.	Fear of seeing and remembering. Trauma. Not grounded and safe. Panic of environment. Fantasy safer.	I learn from all life experiences. I am intrigued with everything and everyone. I integrate life. I am safe now and heal my inner child.
Migraine	Indigestion, colon blockage, lymph toxins, gall bladder and liver issues, protein indigestion.	Intense rage suppressed, indecision, desire that others change, victim, ego not matching true self, if only thoughts.	I flow with life. I welcome relationships and enjoy the variety of experience they bring.

Problem area	Physical Symptoms or Contributors	Emotional Mental Symptoms	Affirmations
Pancreas	Digestion of sugars. Insulin issues. Stress in life.	Worry, bitterness, critical, fear, need to please, shame, Lack of trust.	I trust God fully. I love being an instrument in God's hands. I relax and do my best.
Sciatica	Hip and jaw. Greens, Calcium, Magnesium, friendly flora, colon.	Overwhelm with relationships, money issues, no joy, fear of future.	I let go of the past and make room for a great future. I learn from life. Life is a great adventure. I let others be, I let myself be true to me.
Sinus	Infection in ear, jaw, glands. Small intestine digestion issues. Lack of quality bacteria in gut. Inflammation in gut and head. TMJ jaw, cranial sphenoid stress.	Self-pity, self-hate, anger to self, grief and regret, depressed, lonely, stuck, worried, Root chakra is not grounded, analytical, worried.	I love life as it is. I hope and act and let God do the rest. I honor and respect myself. I let go of any and all resentments. The future is bright.
Skin Rashes	Toxicity of blood, lymph and colon. Inflammation of gastro-intestinal lining. Fats not digested or assimilated.	Itching to do something. Suppressed rage or hatred. Fear of going forward or speaking truth. Panic with living truth.	I flow with my desires and goals. I take my time and enjoy life. I let go of resentments to all people. I can be true to me and others. I speak my truth. I trust life.

Problem area	Physical Symptoms or Contributors	Emotional Mental Symptoms	Affirmations
Small Intestines	Lack of quality flora. Harsh diet. Need of fiber, enzymes, greens. Less wheat and sugar. Stress and worry.	Not assimilating life. Learning and short-term memory. Worry and fear. Suppressed anger.	I open to learn in all situations and all people. I respect myself and I am teachable.
Spleen	Blood toxicity, liver toxicity, immune system compromised, fatigue.	Bitterness, need to please, pushing to excel, driven.	I balance my life. I am real with who I am. I can filter what is not mine. I am safe.
Stomach	Lack of good gut flora. pH imbalance. Lack of hydrochloric acid. Digestion issues.	Lack of Trust. Satisfaction issues. Personal power.	I am grateful for every moment of life and my experience. I respect myself and my gifts. I stand up for myself.
Thyroid	Excess physical and emotional stress. Poor diet. Binge eating. Hormonal stress.	Worry. Mistrust. Desperate feelings. Hopelessness. High expectations not fulfilled.	I trust God. I enjoy the events and people in my life. I balance wishes with reality.

Problem area	Physical Symptoms or Contributors	Emotional Mental Symptoms	Affirmations
Ulcers	Adrenal stress, excess adrenal, noradrenaline, excessive use of cortisol, lack of fiber, excessive carbohydrates.	Going faster than your heart and mind can handle. Stress in the aura and chakras. Mistrust. Personal relationship stresses with finances and close associations.	I run and walk in synchronization with life. I am safe to be. Money is my friend. I can slow down and work through this. God wants the best for me. I give myself permission to feel what is best. I trust my intuition.
Weight	Indigestion. Hormonal fluctuations. Inflammation and toxicity. Dietary and lifestyle issues.	Hatred to self or others. Fear of others. Clutter in heart and mind. Greed. Determined to have it all without the letting go of something secret. Living to eat.	I can let go of my favorite food. I enjoy eating to live. I love myself. I can respect my body by eating what is great for me.

Emotionally and Mentally Based
Bio-Fire Alarms

Emotionally and Mentally based *bio-fire alarms* and their possible meanings:

Problem area	Physical Symptoms	Emotional/Mental Symptoms	Affirmations
Anger	Protein indigestion. Anger may show in the jaw, back, heart, liver or lymph. Sometimes in diabetes, arthritis, cancer, or skin problems.	Suppressed fear. Fear of losing control. Need of holding personal space. Loss of Respect of others.	I love life. I am in control. I trust the universe. I allow others to be themselves. My desires are fulfilled with respect and cooperation. Everyone is my teacher.
Anxiety	Protein indigestion. Excess adrenaline or norepinephrine. Abdominal muscle constriction. Lower Chakra lessened. Higher Chakras stressed. Low Blood sugar.	Fear of future. Less ability to discern past events with current concerns. Breathing in lower abdominals.	I am safe. It is okay to be afraid, I give myself permission to feel. I give myself permission to let go and enjoy.

Problem area	Physical Symptoms or Contributors	Emotional Mental Symptoms	Affirmations
Bitter	Liver, Gall Bladder, Lymph, Joints, Muscles.	Bitter herbs are cleansers to the body. Difficult experiences are to be teaching times. Excess bitter is the holding on to what should have or should not have been. Resenting self, others, and events and not allowing understanding and healing.	I learn from all my experiences. I let life's painful events mold, shape, and refine me into a better human being. I enjoy all the aspects of life including the bitter/sweet.
Blame	Liver, Gall Bladder, Bladder, and Colon issues. Fat and protein digestion. Low or High Blood sugar.	Frustration with self and others. Often from a lack of control. Wanting to keep life the way it was or should be. Trying to force the issue. Not enjoying what is. Fear of responsibility. Wishing to be acknowledged.	I let go of the need to control. I am in control of inner self. I ask and receive what is best for me. I enjoy what is. I flow.

Problem area	Physical Symptoms or Contributors	Emotional Mental Symptoms	Affirmations
Depression	Hormonal fluctuation. Carbohydrate indigestion. Lack of fiber and good balanced diet. Liver and colon blockages. Lymphatic issues. Thyroid, adrenal, blood sugar, emotional stresses.	Suppressed anger. Suppressed sadness. High expectations unfulfilled. Hopelessness. A need to be right about an event, a person, or feeling.	I hold onto joy, love, and expressions of laughter and sharing. I let go of grief, if only, it shouldn't have been, and it is hopeless. I am hope and life is a great teacher and opportunity.
Desperate	Lung and adrenals. Low on oxygen, sugar, calcium, and electrolytes. Blockage of fluids.	Craving for things that don't match inner values. Not surrender to higher will or understanding. Fear of past affecting future.	I enjoy surprises. I want to try new things. I hope and act for the best and accept what comes to me. I attract confidence. I attract insight and understanding.
Despondent	Liver and colon sluggishness. Indigestion of fats. Male/female hormonal fluctuations.	Past events are not in the personal agenda or plan. Controlling is priority. Frustration.	I have opportunity to learn from life's changes. I encourage spontaneity and adventure.

Problem area	Physical Symptoms or Contributors	Emotional Mental Symptoms	Affirmations
Embarrassed	Minerals and Trace Mineral deficiency. Low and High Blood Pressure and Sugar. Trapped bacteria or other similar agents.	Need to hide inner self. To protect the self from being hurt.	I want to be real. I have an opportunity to share myself and enjoy connecting with other people who share themselves.
Entitlement	Throat sacral plexus, and solar plexus energy fluctuations. Imbalanced liver, thyroid, heart, and sexual organs.	Major or minor abusive relationships can breed entitlement. The feeling I deserve is healthy if not at the expense of others. There is deep seeded resentment of others. Shame and guilt.	I deserve the best and enjoy creating it with integrity. I want others to receive the best while respecting myself. My inner child opens to be nourished in a positive safe way.
Fear	Kidney, Bladder, Heart. Chakras are not balanced. Sugars out of balance. Protein assimilation.	Wishing but not acting. Deep issues of lack of control. Hurt and pain from past. Fear of future.	I am a good person. I am the best I can be today. I enjoy creating and progressing at a pace that is safe and beneficial. Fear is a gift. I turn obstacles into stepping stones.

Problem area	Physical Symptoms or Contributors	Emotional Mental Symptoms	Affirmations
Frustration	Liver, jaw, sinus, colon, small intestines, sexual organs, headaches, muscle aches.	High expectations not fulfilled. Blame to others and events. Dreams not lasting and not satisfied with what comes to you.	I welcome the challenges of life. Resistance is a gift that strengthens me and it turns into a positive force for good and forward motion. God open my heart and strengthen my liver.
Grief	Heart problems, lung problems, candida or yeast overgrowth. Mind chatter.	Not able to process through life's events. Stuck. Thoughts of "if only" and "should".	I open to see the gifts of the past, let go and make room for understanding, wisdom and deep joy.
Guilt	Small intestines, sexual organs, kidney, colon, and immune system. Food sensitivities.	Self-blame and criticism becoming a major focus. Not allowing for the human side of self. Not focusing on positive benefits from experiences.	I am a good and likeable person. I love myself. I am doing the best I can. I focus on the positive benefits from my experiences.

Problem area	Physical Symptoms or Contributors	Emotional Mental Symptoms	Affirmations
Judgmental	Liver and gall bladder issues. Joints and lymph.	Criticism leads to many diseases of the body, mind and soul. Judgment with forgiveness leads to wisdom. Judgment with negative emotion leads to loneliness, sadness, anger, frustration. It leads to spiritual and mental blindness.	I open my eyes to see all possibilities. I welcome the views and perceptions of others. Everyone is my teacher. All things work for my good. I let go of emotional baggage.
Lazy	Colon problems, allergies, digestive issues.	Lack of purpose or mission. Loss of will to someone else. Traumatized and then suppressed. Dessert of inaction is greater than the fruit of passion.	I am curious. I experiment with new things daily. I refuse to take things personally. I am independent to choose my life instead of waiting for others to do it for me. The path of life is more fun than watching it go by.

Problem area	Physical Symptoms or Contributors	Emotional Mental Symptoms	Affirmations
Overwhelm	Dehydration, electrolytes, sugar imbalance. Adrenal and lungs.	Fearing outcomes before they have a chance to develop. Breathing in fear rather than faith and courage. Fear of pain, fear of failure, and other fears for self or for others. Trusting is a scary thing. Adventure and fun are foreign concepts.	I stop taking the fears of others. I take responsibility for myself and let others take responsibility for themselves. I breathe openly and fully. I let the burdens of life go and send them to God. I trust God and life.
Obnoxious	In need of quality fats from fish, flax, and other quality oil based foods. Exercise. Toxins. Dehydration.	Desire for attention. Fear of being trapped but desperate for acceptance. Bored. If you are judging the other as obnoxious you need to read the judgment entry.	I move my body and my mind as one. I am clear about my intentions. I find enjoyment in learning and work. I consider the feelings of others.

Problem area	Physical Symptoms or Contributors	Emotional Mental Symptoms	Affirmations
Panic	Carbohydrate indigestion. Stomach and small intestines stress. Adrenal overload. Dehydration.	Thinking: that event should not have occurred. Not able to love what is happening. Wishing for different results. Confusing current and traumatic events.	I give myself permission to be here. I take life one moment at a time. I love what is.
Rage	Digestive issues. Don't chew my food. Protein digestion. Liver blockage. Lymph.	Suppressed emotions have to surface sometime. Often rage uncovers depression, sadness, overwhelm, panic, and pain. Rage is a need to set a boundary.	I take this opportunity. Life is a gift. Life is my teacher. I am grateful. I choose to easily let my frustrations go.
Sadness	Liver sluggishness. Eating too many carbohydrates.	Grief that is unresolved. Fear that is unresolved. Suppressed anger. Not grounded positively.	This too shall pass. I welcome tears of healing enabling me to grow flowers of newness.

Problem area	Physical Symptoms or Contributors	Emotional Mental Symptoms	Affirmations
Scattered	Sugar and Carbohydrate indigestion. Fat indigestion. Liver Bile blockage. Insulin issues. Dehydration. Candida or yeast.	Not able to focus. Non-cohesiveness. Lack of true identity. Fear of self. Fear of future. Absorbing others feelings. Loss of purpose.	I choose life. I choose to see and experience what is now. I like to focus on what is fun. I am safe to be here now.
Terror	Shock in nerves. Vitamin B complex. Detoxification of endogenous and exogenous toxins needed.	Sensory integration dysfunction. Meditation, energy, body work, grounding needed.	I create a safe environment. I integrate my sensory world to flow with my environment.
Unworthy	Sluggishness of body fluids. Imbalance in heart, liver, colon and sexual organs.	Fear of other's and God's retribution. A need to be perfect even to breathe and survive. Mistakes become the focus rather than success. Worth is not about self-value determined by the doings of life. Worth is about your true essence of who you really are: a child of God. You are a light, let yourself shine your uniqueness.	I am worth. I couldn't breathe without God's energy. I have the capacity receiving and sharing love, ideas, friendship and more. I forgive myself. I allow myself to be human. I turn mistakes into experiments.

Positive Emotional and Mental States with Affirmations

Area	Physical Aspect	Emotional/Mental Aspect	Affirmations
Action	Balanced physical body with emotional body.	Able to complete the creation cycle. First the idea, intent, faith, planting, action, harvesting. Action that is not based on denial and is based on clarity and desire which attracts energy, ideas, and more success.	I enjoy the work of life. I take curiosity and faith mix it with ideas and act upon them. I enjoy the fruit. I enjoy the dessert of labor and use it for the seeds of more action and experience.
Adventure	Balanced "seeking system" in the brain.	Safe risk is a treat of life. Adventure adds zest to life.	I am full of adventure and intrigue. Life brings me awesome energy and I give it back with adventure.
Beauty	Balanced elimination system. Balanced eating habits. Balanced digestion. Real beauty is from within.	Balanced self-awareness. Deep inner connection to purpose, values, and God. Attention to detail with appreciation for the purpose.	I am true to my devotion to God, my inner self and my principles. I express beauty in all areas of my life. I honor others and expect respect from others. I enjoy creating. I respect the details within the balance of all areas of life.

Area	Physical Aspect	Emotional/Mental Aspect	Affirmations
Charisma	Balanced cerebellum, chakras, spiritual and heart connection.	Able to create opportunities to share the personality of self and love with others. Respect of others and wanting to share inner passion. Able to be in synchronization with others and with life.	I am in-synchronization with others and life. My smile, view, expression is naturally full of vitality, joy, sharing, adventure, and respect.
Clarity	Balanced brain, lymph, colon, sexual organs, heart.	Able to be congruent between heart, mind, soul, and body. Congruency with goals at all levels.	I am free to be the real me. I see what really is. I am peace and strength. I act now with clear intent and focus. I know my principles and share my life based on these. I attract empowerment for self and others.
Courage	Strong heart, stomach, sexual organs, adrenals, and thyroid.	Able to stand true to principles. There is awareness of who you are, what your values are, and where you are going. Depth of determination and faith. Love of life and wanting to embrace it. Understanding and strength.	I am full of passion for life. I choose my path in alignment with my true purpose and universal will. I defend what is of great value and purpose. I share courage, strength and understanding.

Area	Physical Aspect	Emotional/Mental Aspect	Affirmations
Curiosity	Strong Brain (the connection from the brain stem, limbic, to frontal lobes), heart, small intestines.	Curiosity breeds desire, learning, insight, satisfaction, change, awareness, and transformation. Balanced desire and wisdom is the key to a balanced mind and heart.	I am in awe of nature, people, & the universe. Life is full of fantastic surprises. I yearn to learn more & discover. I share my discoveries with God, family, and friends. I engage others in experimenting life.
Decisive	Balanced Gall Bladder, Liver, Blood, Brain, Lung. Able to digest fats and proteins well.	Able to be clear about purpose, mission, goals, and principles. Clarity is more important than pleasing. Action is more important than fear. Choice is more important than worrying about making a mistake.	I know what I want and I am choice. I decide and seek divine understanding. I am able to change my mind when clear. I am grateful for the opportunity of choosing. I have the courage to choose.

Area	Physical Aspect	Emotional/Mental Aspect	Affirmations
Empathy	Balanced colon, spleen, pancreas, stomach, heart, and pituitary.	Able to see past the pity or anger. Able to see the value of others pains and upsets as lessons to be learned in life. Able to go through pain and grief and embrace the goodness of life.	I respect others and I respect myself. I allow others their pain. I guide others to release their pain but only on their timing and schedule. I allow them space to heal.
Faith	Balanced mind and spirit. Balanced kidney, bladder, small intestines, liver, heart.	Able to believe without seeing absolutely. Able to follow the inner guidance with courage. Not afraid to face the inner critic and doubter. Able to take the first step with hope.	I am confident in God. I am confident in myself. I am confident that life will support me as I support my true values and principles. I believe in truth. I am grateful for intuition and guidance that comes easily with clarity and intention. I am aligned with self, God, and purpose.

Area	Physical Aspect	Emotional/Mental Aspect	Affirmations
Fun	Balanced 5 elements and all organs. Especially the lungs, lymph, heart and the small intestine.	Able to enjoy the moment. A high level of intelligence mixed with non-burden. If not in denial, then able to see and laugh at the game of life and its many paradoxes.	I enjoy the downs & ups of life. I create fun when bored, intense, serious, or in risk. I attract enjoyment and recreation to me. I recreate newness, aliveness, and joy every moment. My life path is fun in all areas.
Hope	Balanced mind, spine, immunity, glands, heart, lymph, blood, cholesterol, and hormones.	Able to see the possibilities of life. Able to reap the light and the divine from every moment. Able enjoy what is. Able to grieve and go on. Able to understand self and others.	I desire to improve and I am satisfied with now. I enjoy wishing and acting on those dreams. I face reality with clarity and wisdom and look forward to new possibilities of opportunities of learning, growth, fun, adventure, and sharing,

Area	Physical Aspect	Emotional/Mental Aspect	Affirmations
Intelligence	Balanced colon, stomach, brain.	The majority of the communication comes from the "gut" to the brain, not the other way around. Intelligence is more than a degree. It is the ability of create associations among the many aspects of life. It is the ability to listen to intuition from the root, sacral plexus, solar plexus, and heart chakras. It is the ability to discern between illusion and reality. It is honest discernment.	I learn from all sources. Everyone is my teacher. All of nature is my teacher. I attract organization and association of ideas within my subconscious and conscious for optimal intelligence. I use God's gift of intelligence for the betterment of self and mankind.
Joy	Balanced kidneys, brain, heart, liver, spleen, stomach. Balanced physical body, mental body. Chakras aligned and flowing.	Able to live fully in the moment. Able to see life as an opportunity instead of a burden. Able to be in curiosity and satisfaction simultaneously.	I am so alive. I feel the earth and heaven in all things. People are amazing. I have passion for living in all areas. I share joy with whoever wants to receive. I respect others where they are and enjoy resistance as an opportunity of understanding.

Area	Physical Aspect	Emotional/Mental Aspect	Affirmations
Laughter	Balanced lungs, colon, heart, liver.	Able to enjoy life despite the obstacles. The dualisms and paradoxes of life and others become the learning mirrors, thus the paradigm shifts and spontaneous humor.	I see the shadows of life as a mirror of my silly judgments and fears. I laugh at the paradox of life and take the awareness as an opportunity to expand insight. I enjoy the multiplicity of patterns that create the paradoxes.
Love	Balanced in all the systems - physical, mental emotional, spiritual. The more love is actualized the greater the energy and vitality.	Love is the basis of all attractions. If the attraction is skewed it is due to a lack of internal congruency. Actualized love is powerful. All emotions are originally based on love. Judgment and pain can twist and alter emotional views. All emotions can be transformed back to its original form if embraced and understood.	I am love. My partner is love. All things and creatures are unique hues from the spectrum of love. The colors of life show me the positive shadows of love. I allow understanding and healing as I embrace my pain from past experiences.

Area	Physical Aspect	Emotional/Mental Aspect	Affirmations
Passion	Balanced sacral plexus with root chakra and other energies. Balanced lower body organs.	Passion is the zest of life. It is the fruit of intelligence, curiosity, love, courage, and worth. One hundred percent Unconditional love is not possible as a human, but to be near the ninety percentile of unconditional love then passion is required. Be creative, forgiving and actively sharing to grow passion. Passion is sensory and feeling based.	I am full of passion for my life mission. I am passionate about my work and play. I dig deep to feel life. I want to be real, connected, focused and experience the moment.
Peace	Balanced kidney, bladder, colon, and lung.	Real peace is the absence of fear and anxiety. Peace is not a denial state but a moment of clarity when the frequencies of life are congruent. Peace may or may not have a feeling. Peace is being at ease either in motion or in stillness.	I attract peace. I express peace. My heart is full of peace. Each day I arise in peace and complete the day in peace. Conflicts of life are opportunities which lead to peaceful completions of understanding and joy.

Area	Physical Aspect	Emotional/Mental Aspect	Affirmations
Trust	Balanced digestion, immunity, and balanced blood sugar.	Able to let faith take hold. Able to be courageous and know that God is always supporting. Able to find some truth in all things and people. Able to let go of judgment of the falsehoods or shadows of others.	I live in fullness. I trust in life, self, my body, others, earth, and God. I experiment with life knowing that I am okay and safe. The future is safe. Life offers support in all areas.

The seed of health & success
is positive, focused attention.

CHAPTER SIX

Centering for Body Weight Reduction

Before addressing body reduction with centering techniques, consider the following information: Recently, it has been shown that adipose tissue contains adipocytes. These cells make up a major neuroendocrine system of the body. In other words, when a person gains excess body weight, it is more than just calories. The fat cells can and do send messenger substances and signals along neural pathways to the brain and the rest of the body.

Adipose tissue can actually be more powerful than most people realize. It may be part of an inflammatory response within a physical neural network. In the past, when individuals claimed that weight had an emotional connection, it was never believed. But now, science is finding that with a neuroendocrine connection, excess fat may in fact alter body function and affect emotions. And the author adds – emotions and intention can affect adipose (fat) tissues. Centering for weight reduction is a powerful tool. (*For additional information consider reading the end of the section on Centered Emotions and the Centered Health and Healing Section*).

The freedom of easily maintaining a desirable weight is wished for by most of us in western society. Simply said, losing weight is a constant issue for most people. Weight gain is dreaded; thus, food is both an enemy and a friend. Diets are rampant, cravings are too. To eat with less stress, as mentioned in this book, is the last thing on most people's minds. To eat, and not gain weight, and maintain self-image is all too often on most people's minds.

If image becomes more important than clarity, joy, and the depth of relationships, then a person is likely addicted to the control of self and perhaps others, through body and food manipulation. What if image was less important? What if image supported your deeper desires of love and connection?

In my work with clients, there is always a deep need for love and acceptance that supersedes their desires to lose weight. When a person does not receive love and connection, they often create other ways of getting that love. One way is through food, or with the obsession of not being able to eat it. Food sometimes becomes an object that replaces real love and nurturing relationships.

One technique for centered weight loss is to focus on creating clarity about the nurturing of your body and your heart. To really feel the love of God, the love from another individual, and self-love toward yourself and your body, is the most powerful way of emotionally creating weight reduction. To want the love and acceptance from another human being is normal. But to crave it deeply can cause a few problems.

For example, Tammy had tried to lose weight with so many diets. Everyone around her was losing weight. She went to the best programs in town but just could not reduce her dress size. One day she found a friend who would walk with her and spend time talking about life, becoming the friend she had always wanted. Suddenly, the weight started to come off. The diets and protein drinks were effective for about eight months and then suddenly the progress ended. Tammy was confused why the weight program was not working again.

After working with Tammy, she admitted that her friend changed her mind overnight about their friendship and the walks were no longer happening. She was devastated. After some probing, her sadness revealed a deep subconscious belief that "If I don't have a friend, then I can't lose weight."

She couldn't believe it. She knew that her conscious mind did not believe that statement but she soon realized that her subconscious mind was fixated on that belief. Then she comprehended that she wanted to find a friend that was nurturing like her mother. Tammy had lost her mother to cancer several years ago. Afterwards, she started eating to fill the void left by the lost. However, when this friend came into her life, the friendship filled the void and she no longer needed the food for love. Yet, when the new friend left her, it was another abandonment that supported her old negative belief. She could not lose weight, and she used food to fill the void.

Once Tammy saw this clearly, she decided that she did not want her goals of weight reduction to be inhibited by the events of her personal friendships. She realized that food was not really about friend-to-friend love. She had known this consciously but did not realize how subtle the belief was in her body. She knew she missed her mom but did not know the extent of her pain. She now knew it was more than just a conscious decision to make a lasting change. As a result, she went through some emotional releasing of sadness and anger, changing of habits, and deep centering techniques to transform the subconscious.

Furthermore, whenever she ate she took a moment to connect to the purpose of the food. She asked herself, is this food for health or for pain control? Is it for personal growth or for body bloating? Is it for the benefit of life and body, or for denial? Defining the action in the moment made a huge difference after she transformed the negative belief.

The following information about emotional conflicts is one of the methods you can use to assist you in transforming the negative beliefs that are sabotaging your efforts.

Healing the Emotional Conflicts of Weight Loss

Usually there is a double mindedness when trying to lose weight. This means that your mind is going in two directions. Indecisiveness from the subconscious will usually cause weight-fullness, not weightless-ness.

Creating the proper state of mind is important. The proper state of mind is not one that is double-minded, confused, upset, or resentful. The body will do what it is told. There are always instructions coming to your body from the autonomic nervous system, but if the nervous system is receiving conflicting thoughts and feelings, it will respond with confusing results in the body. Some of those conflicts may be seeded deep in the subconscious with beliefs that are passed on from generation to generation.

Other conflicts may be current relationship issues that are translated into feelings and beliefs that cause emotionally based eating habits. And lastly, some may be based on trauma or emotional events that caused deep scars etched into the psyche of the heart, creating conflicts between image and safety.

Examples include:

"I want to lose weight but I am not safe around men (or women)"

"I want to regain my youthful looks but it is dangerous out there."

"Eat everything on your plate."

"Don't waste food because of the starving children in other countries."

"If you eat that you will get fat."

"You have no control."

"I'd rather be fat than starve."

"I'd rather starve than be fat."

"I have been so good; I deserve this dessert."

"I want a great body, but I'll never get one."

"I have to eat my ice cream, I deserve it, and when he's gone I need it."

"My soda pop is what keeps me going. I have to have it."

"I can't lose weight no matter what I do."

"Responsibility is scary."

"I have to eat to survive."

"I'd rather be overweight than go on another diet."

"I'd rather be overweight than let my _____ (parent, friend, associate) be right."

Losing weight is more than just a matter of what you do. It is also a matter of what you are. You can try, and try everything; but if the desires of your heart and the logic of your mind are not on the same page, then you will try and try, with very little success. If you have internal conflicts, then weight loss will be slow and laborious.

How do you create congruency of the heart and mind in regards to weight loss? Sometimes the differences and conflicts are resolved by becoming aware and choosing a new integrated path. Often, a simple affirmation, along with deep centering breathing, is enough. However, for deep seated beliefs and emotions, it requires more effort. The gift for that effort is tremendous personal growth while creating fantastic body fat loss.

The following technique will help with conflicting beliefs in regards to weight loss:

1. Breathe in a cleansing breath. Breathe out slowly.

2. Close your eyes. Focus your mind on the heart.

3. Keep your breath slow, and while focusing on your heart, visualize what you desire.

4. If your desire is weight modification, then visualize that.

5. Pause, and be sure to visualize what you want.

6. Breathe deeply into the lower abdominal region.

7. Visualize one of your obstacles (a belief or habit) that is blocking the path to losing body fat.

8. Let the obstacles take shape and form in your mind. (If you cannot imagine the shape, then draw it on a piece of paper, then do the visualization).

9. Keep your breath slow and focused.

10. Visualize the shape or form having a mouth.

11. Let the shape or form speak.

12. Ask the shape what its purpose is. (or ask "What are you trying to give to me by blocking my path to weight loss?")

13. Whatever the answer, acknowledge it. Do not argue with yourself. The answer is a belief based on emotions that may not be logical.

14. If there is no reply, then either ask again or choose to send the visual of the obstacle to the sun, to the universe, or to God, to transform it, with the intention of going forward without that obstacle blocking your path).

15. If there is a reply and if the purpose is negative, then ask: what is the positive purpose for this obstacle.

16. Be sure to breathe deeply, slowly and to stay focused.

17. Usually, the obstacle has one of the following purposes:

    a. Defending you from harm.

    b. Creating a diversion from pain or embarrassment.

    c. Not wanting you to starve.

    d. Taking responsibility so you don't have to.

    e. Hiding painful memories to protect you.

    f. Trying to get a message through to you and not knowing how.

    g. And many other possibilities.

18. Once you know the purpose, decide whether to keep the obstacle.

19. If you choose to let it go then wrap it with love, it really was attempting the task of assisting you.

20. Breathe deeply in your body.

21. Breathe out the visualization of the obstacle, and let it go to the universe to be transformed into something that will assist you.

22. Breathe deeply.

23. Ask yourself what has the resistance of this obstacle done for you?

24. What character traits have you created because of this and other obstacles?

25. Breathe out old judgment and resentment.

26. Breathe in gratitude and new resolve.

27. You choose to start a new life. Choose a life of responsibility, not based on fear, but based on the ability to respond without the need for obstacles trying to protect you. You can still be safe and be nourished.

28. Breathe deeply and affirm:

    a. I am safe.

    b. I am nourished.

    c. I love myself.

    d. I am fun.

    e. I enjoy eating what is great for my body.

This technique is powerful. If you need additional assistance, seek out a professional psychotherapist, hypnotherapist, or another healing professional. Consider taking some of the classes offered at LivebyHeart.com to learn techniques to assist in your path to your desired weight. Also, reread the sections in this book about the heart and mind and the emotional processing information.

Weight loss is really an opportunity to connect to the parts of yourself that you have ignored for years. How much is your little child-self wanting to play and enjoy life? Or is the child feeling guilty? Is this inner child trying to get instant gratification with food? Is this child using the sedentary lifestyle to escape some important truth or responsibility? Actually, your inner child is much more satisfied when she/he feels taken care of properly.

Satisfaction starts with being safe and loved. And that starts with deep understanding and wisdom, honoring self, and showing self-respect.

Most individuals who really understand the purpose of their obstacles and see the gifts of those obstacles, are able to turn their lives around and see spontaneous change. The subconscious inner child and the conscious adult start working together instead against each other.

Use these centering techniques:

1. Release the old physical and emotional pain.

2. Integrate the pieces and parts.

3. Build the inner strength to eat and live fully, and most importantly,

4. Create the inner motivation of living in joy and completeness.

As you use this and other similar processes, you will begin to become aware of habits and thoughts that are spontaneously affecting your progress. When you see, hear, and sense these epiphanies or "ah-hah's", respect them. These are windows of understanding in your subconscious that allow you to make a change in the moment. These moments of change will affect the obsessive, functional parts of the brain for good. These moments of change should not be filled with guilt and self-blame, but with excitement and enthusiasm. The positive emotions can help store positive behavioral change.

Hugs for Weight Reduction

Sometimes it is nice to find a simple technique; something that doesn't require a lot of effort. Hugs for Weight Reduction are just that. Most people with weight issues have a deep-seated need for safe affection and love. Often the body protects itself from that love, while desperately seeking affection, and emotional and physical love.

Starting with Hugs is a simple, but safe option. You can use a simple hug several times a day from many people. Often a person cannot find another individual that can give unconditionally for a few moments a week. It does not have to be unconditional love all day long, just a few moments a day. *A hug a day gives some pounds away.*

I know some people who say, "I get lots of hugs and the inches still grow". However, most hugs are given with some hidden agendas. Some of these hidden agendas could be: "I wish you'd love me more," "I will give if you give," "I worry about you so much," "I need you so much," "I just want you to feel me," "I just want you to understand how I feel," "I hope you will _____," (fill in the blank).

These and many other thoughts and feelings can be hidden behind a hug and the emotional nourishment that people exchange. If so, the hug is not unconditional and does not qualify for "a hug a day keeps some pounds away". Sharing and caring is not the same as carrying the pain of others. Deep emotional release and balancing is particularly important for those with the type of weight gain that is attached to issues of martyrdom.

The female brain is highly wired for satisfaction via touch, that provides nourishment to the core of the heart; in other words, unconditional love from the heart. When a female receives deep caring and understanding, the body sends fewer stress messages to the hypothalamus. Then, satiety (the state of being satisfied, i.e. for food) messages are sent from the ventromedial nucleus of the hypothalamus to the body.

In simple terms, that translates to less cravings. Less cravings means there are fewer grabby sensations for those fattening carbohydrates, allowing the body to rest between meals. You will desire more protein and quality fats for body strengthening and building.

Procedure:

1. Find three people that you can hug.

2. Obtain their permission to give and receive hugs, with no expectation whatsoever.

3. Get at least three hugs a day for 31 days.

4. The hugs should last for 2 minutes.

5. The first thirty seconds, both people send equal amounts of energy intensity.

6. The next minute you hug normally. The person receiving the hug relaxes and does not hug back with the same intensity.

7. Visualize light or positive energy going to that person. This light is divine light or God's light. You are just a messenger; it is not your energy. Let it be God's.

8. The next minute you receive the hug while you relax and do not send back the same intensity of hug.

9. Visualize you receiving divine energy or God's energy with light and love. Love is the only true healer and communicator. Light is one of the pathways of love.

Receive love without any agendas. Let yourself be given love, caring, and understanding.

10. The last thirty seconds both people hug with equal intensity.

The more you do this process, the more powerful it is. It is even more powerful if you choose to let go of expectations of weight loss, as well as letting go of expectations from the other person. This is just an experience. Enjoy life. Allowing yourself to trust, is the key to this technique. The gift of this technique is far more than body weight manipulation. It opens the door to so many wonderful experiences with energy to and from the body, intuition, communication, and more.

This procedure works best if you do not absorb the pain, worries and conflicts of other people. If you let the little girl or little boy inside feel safe and nourished, then the body will crave less. If you start to crave food more with this technique, then you are activating emotions that might need some processing.

When you work through the emotions and stored pain, the expression of hugging is empowering for both parties. It represents deep respect and connection. Let the hugging lead you to deep discussions and heart level communication with someone each day. This will honor the body at the next level of love and acceptance.

Emotional Weight Reduction Affirmations

Affirmations are powerful when combined with centering techniques. When affirmations are aligned and congruent with your heart, mind, and soul, they can change your life and your body. In the work done by Dr. Emoto, he found that affirmations, spoken or written, can and do affect the crystallization patterns of water.

Negative affirmations that people tell themselves, like "I am overweight" or "I am no good" or "No one will love me", have a negative effect on the water and the vibration of the body. The effect is immediate. However, he found that with positive affirmations like, "I am healthy", "I am on the path of healing", or "I love myself", that the crystal nature of the water became beautiful, and the taste of the water changed. We are mostly water; therefore, our entire body is affected instantly by our thoughts, intents and emotions.

Where do those critical, negative affirmations come from? The body is full of cellular memory. Some of the thoughts could be passed down. Other thoughts can come from a higher level of the limbic brain that is wired to judge your circumstances to protect you from harm. Some women have been hurt or abused, so the body may choose to send negative affirmations to keep the woman overweight as a protection. It also can come from a deficit of love as mentioned above, and this lack leads to negative internal affirmations that support those beliefs.

Those beliefs are not necessarily true. However, pain and history create the illusion that they are true. Do you really want to follow a belief that you justify by your past? Is it possible to re-create your present and future with new positive and supportive beliefs?

Search deeply within. Seek to gradually transform the beliefs, emotions, and events that sabotage your life. Find professional assistance to assist you through your process of deep-seated emotional blocks and negative beliefs. Start each day with hope, clarity, fun, joy and other positive feelings and thoughts. Gradually and surely, your life can change, both in the sculpting of your body and in your heart and soul.

The fears of being hurt and embarrassed, of anger and frustration, are just stuck energies. Stuck energies do not have to be your friend. You can find beliefs, habits, experiences, friends and more that support a safe and healthy body and lifestyle. I am in awe of the powerful life changes in those who choose to trust in the transformation process. When a person becomes centered within, the universe and God bring new opportunities for assistance, for change, and for joy.

Choose from the following weight loss affirmations. You can use them with any one of the centering techniques, including visualizations, emotional processing, etc. REMEMBER – as you process and re-create your beliefs, store them with positive emotions, and with passion and energy. Positive emotions will help secure the positive desires.

I love myself today and enjoy body fat reduction every day.

I love my body and my body loves me.

I love it when I wear a size ___.

I am so excited when I eat great and good food.

I am peaceful and clear inside when I eat quality food.

I am safe when I weigh ____.

I am strong, with a trim and slim body.

I am safe with a trim and slim body.

I release the need to hold onto past pain and sufferings.

I release the need to hold onto cravings and false expectations.

I release the need to be resentful of others.

I release the need to hold onto body clutter.

I release clutter in my life, in my body, in my mind, in my surroundings.

God gives me permission to be slim.

I give myself permission to be slim and trim.

I give myself permission to look beautiful.

I give myself permission to enjoy food and push away food that stresses my body.

I am a good person with hopes, and I create a wonderful body and life.

I deserve the best. The best is my desirable weight.

I deserve to be slim and healthy.

I release the false beliefs about weight loss.

I release the belief that size equals power.

I choose the size of my meals, my weight, my body.

I eat with healthy feelings.

I release the need to eat emotionally.

I nurture myself today with 100% love and caring.

I am the best I can be.

I am desirable.

I surround myself with great people who love, support, respect and honor me.

I turn past pain and resentments into understanding and strengths.

I create a life of integrity and creativity.

I love myself as I am now. I am doing the best I can.

I love myself as I follow my heart and mind to reduce weight.

I love myself as I take action.

I love myself.

I lose weight for me.

I enjoy life and myself.

I enjoy it when I take care of myself.

My body and I are great buddies.

I turn fear into courage.

I turn shame into personal opportunity for change.

I transform personalizing others' views into reality and self-respect.

I love my new me.

I am beautiful.

As you go through your weight loss programs, use visualizations every single day. Most people who do lose weight see the possibility in their mind's eye long before the weight comes off. People who doubt the possibility, don't visualize it and get easily frustrated.

The mind is so powerful. If the mind is holding the image subconsciously that a certain size needs to be maintained, then the body will follow the internal subtle commands. Eventually it will become a habit.

Again, if a person with hope and determination includes visualization with their weight loss plans, the body will eventually follow the vision and meet their demands.

Meditation for Balanced Weight Centering

My body is a gift. I treat it with respect.

My body is safe. I am rooted in self-confidence.

My body is functional. I digest food with satisfaction.

My body is whole. I honor all parts of myself.

My body is attractive. I sustain its beauty.

My body is a temple. I experience life as a gift.

My body is soulful. I connect with my inner self.

My body loves life. I eat to maintain that experience.

My body digests and assimilates. I love protein and good fats.

My body is hopeful. I recharge with excitement daily.

My body is resonant. I am energetic and vibrant.

My body is expressive. I am an adventure.

My body shares love. I respect mutual kindness.

My body is fantastic. I shine and reflect joy.

My body is flowing. I move with ease.

My body likes taste. I savor good food for me.

My body is enjoyable. I enjoy sculpting and thinning.

My body is selective. I cherish small amounts.

My body is wonderful. I am magnificence today.

My body is gratitude. I thank God for letting my body reflect goodness, beauty, balance, joy, light, and the other gifts of the universe. May I honor my body and all other people with your light now and always.

Congruency of the heart is the integrity of the soul.

CHAPTER SEVEN

Centering for Nourishing the Body

Eating right, the Centered way, is an act of honoring the body with the foods that show respect to the environment within the body and not just the taste buds. A healthy blend of vegetables, fruits, grains and proteins is a must for health and centered living. By eating a variety of colors of vegetables and fruits, the body will be getting the antioxidants, vitamins, minerals and phytochemicals it needs.

Different nutrients are in each of the varieties of foods represented by color. A variety of colors is good for the body and for enjoyment. Also, when the eye is aesthetically pleased, the body produces supportive energy and chemicals for digestion and assimilation, as well as spiritual support for the quest of the centered life within the physical body.

In order to support the body during the natural ebb and flow of stress and emotions, consider the following suggestions:

1. When stressed, don't eat.

2. However, if you do eat when stressed then eat foods that are easy to digest, i.e. slightly cooked vegetables, soft vegetables, and fruits.

3. When stressed, if you eat, chew slowly. Breath with the intention of releasing and not having the food solve your problems.

4. Avoid excess protein, caffeine and alcohol in times of stress.

5. Avoid sugar and excess carbohydrates. These feed your emotional side in a negative way, creating a vicious cycle of solving problems with quick fixes now, and added weight, later. Quick fixes will lead to anxiety or depression. It means that you don't want to confront an emotional issue and/or you want to take a pseudo form of love instead of responsible love and fullness.

6. Eat smaller meals and take the time to eat slowly. If on the run, eat simply or not at all.

7. Drink lots of water. Eight or more glasses a day.

8. Eat foods with electrolytes and magnesium. Electrolytes are burned during stressful times and are necessary for cellular processes. Magnesium is used by every cell of the body and helps relax muscles. Good sources of magnesium include whole grains, legumes, vegetables, seaweeds, nuts and seeds. Electrolytes include potassium, sodium, magnesium and other trace elements. Foods include- dark green leafy vegetables, oranges, nuts, bananas, kelp, celery, watermelon, asparagus and avocadoes. (Organic foods are preferable because of higher mineral content and lower chemical usage).

9. To prepare for stress, get Omega-3, 6 and 9's in flax seed oil, salmon, fish, borage oil and walnuts.

10. Get a healthy source of phytoestrogens instead of the unhealthy environmental estrogens that are found in

some drugs and chemicals like: hormonal replacements, oral contraceptives, vinyl chlorides, dioxins, PCBs, phthalates (plastics), phenols, and hormones in animal products. The healthy phytoestrogens are the isoflavones from beans, peas, clover, alfalfa, kudzu; lignans from flaxseed, rye, wheat, and sea vegetables; and certain flavonoids from citrus fruits and grapes.

11. Getting a healthy source of B-vitamins is always important. Grains are a good source. Even proper pro-biotics (high quality acidophilus bacteria) helps the body help itself produce B vitamins, and assists the colon and liver with proper detoxification. Higher quality grains like spelt, amaranth, quinoa, sprouted grains, millet will be more supportive and less allergenic. For those with sensitivities to grain (gluten intolerance – use sprouts of seeds and nuts, also greens and quality meats).

12. Take the proper combinations of minerals, vitamins and antioxidants A, C and E so the body can produce its own antioxidants. Also, include alpha lipoic acid, mixed carotenoids, selenium, curcumin, N-acetylcysteine, green tea catechins, lycopene and flavonoids.

13. Trace minerals are essential for health. All chemical processes for your health need the enzymatic cofactors that minerals and trace minerals provide. The body is an electrical and chemical unit. Trace minerals are a part of the bridge for the electrical energy charge to connect life within for healing and living. An additional note: Fatigue and associated health issues have increased since the farmers have not been replenishing the soil with all the traces minerals.

14. Add high quality plant enzymes to your diet. If the body is stressed, the body puts energy into survival and not food

digestion. Enzymes are vital for maintaining a centered physical life. If food digestion is impaired it affects all areas of life - physical, emotional, mental and spiritual. The processed foods in the grocery stores are depleted of nutrients and enzymes. Without the enzymes, the body is forced to use up its precious stores of endogenous enzymes. When there are minimal or no enzymes, food is not easily digested and your health suffers. Enzymes are the basis of digestion and assimilation. (For more information, see your natural health practitioner, or look on LivebyHeart.com, about high-quality enzymes or digestion support ideas).

15. Enjoy eating and honoring the body with wholesome, organic food. Food that has been denatured by chemicals, long shelf life, radiation, or is un-naturally altered, pulls valuable negative ions and positive vital energy from your body.

The next section reviews the centered ways to eat your food so that it will be used optimally for your health.

Centered Dining

"To eat or not to eat, that is the question." What if the question was "to eat in peace, or not to eat in peace?" Most individuals have no idea what they are consuming. The food goes in so fast that the experience involves bulk and speed.

When the body eats without focused attention on the action, the brain brings up past memories and the body tastes the food of the past, feels the food of the past and even brings up the emotions experienced while eating those foods in the past. Because many dinner table experiences are filled with stress, children grow up with thoughts and feelings of stress associated with food. (No wonder the fast food environment was created, no one wanted to feel the confusion and pain that accompany eating.)

Experiencing the joy of true satisfaction, and taste sensations in the present moment, are dwarfed by memories, scattered anxiousness and stressful worries. The body adds these stresses to the associated memories of the food held in the cells of the stomach and the small intestines.

If the mealtime is full of stress, neuro-peptides are produced that correspond with stress, fear, anxiety or anger. If the meal is full of wholeness, communication and calmness, the body continues to function in the parasympathetic nervous system and easily produces the enzymes and acids necessary for proper digestion.

You can clear up sensitivities to foods and life by relaxing and focusing on the dining moment. There is no such thing as Fast Dining. Dining is calm, collected, peaceful, enjoyable and especially satisfying. Good relationships with food and people also enhance the experience. Start making mealtime – dining time.

Technique:

1. Take a deep cleansing breathe after *sitting down* to eat.

2. Say a prayer or affirmation that is a *blessing* to *your body* and to the *food.*

3. Continue in a meditation that is full of gratitude for the food and for the fullness of life.

4. Focus on your food while breathing slowly and calmly.

5. Chew your food long and slow.

6. End the dining experience with a feeling of Gratitude and of Completion.

Centering with Laughter

It is interesting to see the serious attitude of some individuals who claim they want to be happy. The inevitable pain of life does not have to supersede the possibility for happiness. The frustrations of unmet expectations do not have to cloud the gift of a spring day. Harboring resentments can taint relationships and life. Bring in some fun and laughter. Transforming your life brings hope and joy.

Real satisfaction can be felt in the solar plexus. This area of trust and laughter includes the stomach, pancreas, spleen and possibly the duodenum. When you believe that things are never good-enough, there is no room for satisfaction. There is only room for the thoughts and feelings of "if only", "never enough", "worry", "can't wait", anxiety and mistrust. You create a dinner plate with thoughts and feelings that are not very tasty or satisfying.

Consider the delicious meal of trust, giggles, smiles, smirks, chuckles and snickers. The body definitely assimilates laughter much better than worry. Several years ago, Max Skousen introduced humor to the author as part of his healing path.

A profound teacher, Max believed in laughing at his own mistakes, fears, negative self-talk and sabotages. He could see the bigger picture and chuckle at the silliness of taking transformation and centering too seriously. Life Centering is an adventure.

Use some of the breathing techniques to calm the solar plexus, the center area around the upper abdomen. During part of the meditation, visualize soft yellow and see yourself as a child, playing and laughing. Visualize laughing with those you love or send warm flowing energy to the solar plexus.

Open your thoughts to the wisdom of chuckling at your seriousness. Lighten your burden; laugh at your conflicting beliefs and intensity of living. You will be amazed how wonderfully powerful laughter can be.

Humor lightens, Gratitude realigns, Joy sweetens

CHAPTER EIGHT

Centering for Flexibility

There is a tremendous amount of energy that flows through the body. The millions of simultaneous transactions that transpire every moment boggle the conscious mind, but are commonplace for the autonomic mind.

The visible wiring and transportation systems of the body (blood, lymph, nervous system) have been diagrammed by western science; the other non-visible wiring of the human body (acupuncture meridians and chakras) was mapped by Eastern medical practitioners many centuries ago. An acupuncturist uses the energetic pathways of the body for healing. The Chinese and Hindu people have long used this information for meditation.

Accessing this energy in conjunction with moving and stretching the body is beneficial to all the systems of the body.

Hand Mudras and Modes

You can direct the energy of your breath and intention by using finger modes. This is a very powerful way to facilitate fresh oxygen and energy to flow to the colon, heart, small intestines, glands or other organs, depending on which finger the thumb is touching during the breathing and centering technique.

165

In addition to sending energy more directly into a certain area of the body, you can use intentions, affirmations and guided imagery to enhance the experience.

The following is a list of hand mudras, or finger placements. These modes enhance the flow of energy into particular areas. Place the thumb pad against the finger pad. Most of these modes require the fingers to be extended.

In the next section, you will find a more extensive list with more detailed understanding. These modes are to be used with **Life Centering Breathing and Awareness.**

For Breath/Diaphragm Emotional connection – on each hand, hold the ring finger tip to the thumb tip, with the other fingers curled into the palm.

Emotions – ring finger tip to thumb tip, other fingers extended.

Oxygen Enhancement - all fingertips alongside the thumb.

Spiritual mode - the ring and little fingertips to the thumb, other fingers extended.

Focus and Concentration – interlace all the fingers and thumbs. For creative and deeper meditation start the interlocking with the left thumb on top. For a more mental and less mindful experience start with the right thumb on top.

Prayer and Centering Mudra – place the palms flat together. This helps neutralize yin and yang energies.

To focus the energy toward specific organs, chakras, muscles, etc., hold the mode and either place the hands in the desired area and/or visualize the desired organ, chakra, etc. For example, to focus on the small intestines hold the thumb pad to the little finger on one hand and place the other hand over the abdomen while focusing your attention on the organ. Do calm, deep breathing and meditation.

Suggestion: Touch your tongue to the palate of the mouth while breathing in and lower the tongue while breathing out while doing this technique. Insights in the chart are discussed in the book Meditation as Medicine.

Life Centering Breathing for Heart & Body Awareness

In a crazy world of mixed signals and misunderstandings from others and within, I have found this procedure to be effective and clearing. It helps to clear the mind, soften the heart, ground the soul and calm the emotions.

Whether a person is anxious, depressed, overwhelmed or sluggish, it can bring you back to yourself. Often, conflict and stress arise when you are unaware of the mixed messages coming from your mind, your heart, and your body.

Focused attention using these procedures brings the mind back to center. For those with an understanding of energy alignment and acupuncture meridians, it appears to balance the polarities of the body, or, in other words, the negative and positive electrical polarity fields.

When people are breathing and connecting their mind, heart with their body, these polarity fields are aligned. This makes breathing and thinking clear, easy and flowing. The lungs calm and you will feel a sense of grounding to the earth, thus, to your body.

The next procedure will assist you in bringing balance to these polarities.

Nourish & Connect Breathing Technique

Breathe with one of the previous Life Centering Breathing techniques while holding the *Nourish & Connect mode*. The

Nourish & Connect mode grounds the energy of the body and is nurturing to the lungs.

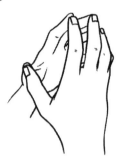

The mode is held as follows: Hold the hands facing each other, with the palms 1″ apart. With the fingers spread apart ¼″, touch each fingertip to their corresponding fingertip on the other hand. Thus, thumb tip to thumb tip, index to index tip, middle to middle tip, ring to ring tip, little finger to little fingertip.

1. Do your chosen breathe technique holding this Nourish & Connect mode for 7 clear and calming breaths.

2. Now take a breath while holding just your Thumb tips together.

3. Breathe while ONLY touching the tips of your Index fingers together.

4. Breathe while ONLY touching the tips of your Middle fingers together.

5. Breathe while ONLY touching the tips of your Ring fingers together.

6. Breathe while ONLY touching the tips of your Little fingers together.

7. Do the **Twist & Connect* mode:

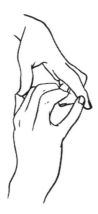

Touch the left Index fingertip to the right Little fingertip, the left Middle finger tip to the right Ring fingertip, the left Ring finger tip to the right Middle finger tip, the left Little fingertip to the right Index fingertip, and the thumb tips together. Take several calming and centering breaths.

8. Come back to the Nourish & Connect mode for 5 to 7 breaths to complete the procedure.

*The **Twist & Connect mode is very soft and deep. It will help with sleep issues when used along with the Nourish & Connect mode. (Be sure to TWIST across and touch the thumb tips while doing the Twist & Connect mode)*

Nourish & Connect may be done several times a day as well as before bed, for a good night's sleep.

The following chart shows the entire procedure with interesting parallels to areas of the body, acupuncture meridians and possible mental or emotional states that could be associated with each. You may enhance the process by allowing the associated thoughts and feelings to flow through you. You may also use visualizations from this book or other procedures to bring more awareness and centering to your body and mind.

Finger	Element and Color	Meridians/ Organs	Insights
1.Nourish & Connect mode*	Earth, Yellow	Spleen and Stomach. Emotions, Hormones.	Helpful, Mindful, Finding Center, Sensitive, Emotional Connection, Completion
2.Thumb tips together	Ether, Space, White	Lungs, Governing Vessel (Du). Neutral, Calm.	Spiritual Connection, Divine Energy, Brain Capacity, Consciousness, Neutralizer, Calming any Manipulation.
3.Index tips together	Air, Metal, Blue	Large Intestines. Physical, Organs.	Physical nature, Ego, Subconscious Energy, Clarity, Motivation
4.Middle tips together	Fire, Orange to Red	Pericardium. Circulation Sex, Nutrition, Glands.	Biochemical nature, Stability, Patience, Warmth, Creation, Creativity
5.Ring tips together	Water, Purple, Lavender	Triple Heater, Adrenals, Thyroid, Emotions, Hormones.	Emotional Power, Personal Power, Energy, Health, Intuition, Immunity, Sensitivity, Patterns of Mind & Heart
6.Little tips together	Wood and Fire, Dk Green, Red	Heart, Small Intestines. Electrical, Energy Meridians.	Intellectual, Activities of Daily Life, Patterns of Energy, Intuitive Communication. Spiritual to Body Aura Link
7.Twist & Connect mode**	Ether, Lt Green, brown, grey	Conception Vessel (Ren), Gall Bladder. Link Etheric to Body.	Duality of Direction or Confusion, Thought, Self, Element's link to the Body, Conception, Weak/Strong, Light/Dark, Truth/Error
8.Nourish & Connect mode*	Earth, Yellow	Spleen and Stomach. Emotions, Hormones.	Helpful, Mindful, Finding Center, Sensitive, Emotional Connection, Completion

All Digit Mode

The All Digit Mode technique helps the lungs to breath naturally deeper into the lower third portion of the organ without force. As mentioned in the Deep Breath discussion most people breath shallowly, up in the highest area of the lungs. Up to two-thirds of your oxygen is assimilated from the lower third of your lungs. Breathing deeper into the lungs automatically makes more oxygen available.

1. Start with your tongue touching the palate of the mouth while breathing in.

2. Take a deep cleansing breath.

3. Start by touching the end of the index fingers of both hands together and slowly breathe.

4. While maintaining the index fingers in position, touch the two middle fingers together and slowly breathe.

5. Now touch the two ring fingers and slowly breathe.

6. Now touch the two little fingers together and slowly breathe.

7. Notice how the breath is slowly moving down the body and becoming deeper with each new finger added.

8. Now touch the two thumbs and slowly breathe.

9. Notice how that provides a nice completion.

Keep the breath moving throughout the body and combine with affirmations and/or visualizations. This will take the centering deeper into the cells and energy fields of the body and the aura.

The Centered Floating Pause

Inhaling and exhaling can have a different effect on two parts of the nervous system. Calmly exhaling helps you release and relax the sympathetic nervous system. Calmly inhaling helps you release any resistance in the parasympathetic nervous system. Both systems affect the organs of the body and their associated "referred" body muscles, which react to your stress levels.

The space between inhaling and exhaling can also have an effect on the nervous system. Notice when you hold your breath with Life Centering meditations, or with any other breathing technique. Do you feel like you are forcing it? Do you feel like you are becoming desperate for another breath of air? If so, then you are activating the sympathetic nervous system (fight or flight).

This technique is called a "forced hold" and is followed with a calming breath. By intentionally engaging the sympathetic nervous system, then immediately calming the body through breath, you are teaching your body how to relax after inducing stress.

However, there is more than one way to hold your breath. A breathing technique I prefer is called a "floating pause." It is a pause in time and space, requiring no effort, causing no stress.

Remember your childhood experience of swinging on the swings at the playground? The floating pause can be likened to that moment of pause in between rising and falling. A blissful moment when you feel a lift in your belly. When you "pause" between breaths, you are in that floating pause state.

You will know when you have reached a floating pause, when the space between inhale and exhale feels natural, effortless and relaxed. Your breath is like an ocean wave, as the water rises, pauses, then rolls into its downward movement.

Practicing the floating pause technique takes time. Most people are accustomed to holding their breath intensely and then pushing their breath out. If you want to over-induce carbon dioxide with a forced holding of the breath, then you may receive a temporary high, but that is not the calmness and bliss that comes with the "floating pause" technique.

You will know that you have not achieved the floating pause if you feel an urgency or tendency to inhale sharply. This is often experienced with a forced hold.

If you are in the practice of using more intense breathing methods currently, like the "forced hold", it may be useful to determine if your body is experiencing stress, and in which nervous system, sympathetic or parasympathetic.

First, let's detect which system is stressed when you hold your breath.

Take a cleansing breath. Then a long inhale and a long exhale.

Now take a long inhale again and hold your breath. Notice what happens. Do you feel an urge in your muscles or in your thoughts to breathe out? For some, their chest or jaw tightens. For others, they begin to feel a bit panicky.

Now, exhale and take another cleansing breath.

If you are experiencing any of these symptoms when holding your breath at the *top* of the inhalation, then you are activating the sympathetic nervous system.

This can indicate several things. Your daily experience is probably fraught with primal emotions and fight or flight reactions. This includes both physical and emotional expression. You could also be eating too many sweets, or not taking enough time to let your body rest to let your muscles settle down. You may have an overwhelming fear of feeling depressed, thus, you could have the temptation to stay busy in your mind to keep yourself in a false-happy state. Or, perhaps you have a fear of relaxation. Anxiety and worry may be your method of keeping you alert so that you are always prepared for what might happen.

Is the stress really worth it?

Now breath in again, and then exhale with a long breath and at the end of the exhale, hold your breath. Notice what happens. Do you feel a desperate need to breathe in now? Do you struggle to breathe in again? Or when you do breathe in, do you hesitate?

In other words, do you feel your lungs hesitate, not knowing when to actually breathe, and possibly causing a little lightheadedness, as if your lungs are unsure, and are waiting for a command?

If you are experiencing these symptoms while holding your breath at the *end* of the exhalation, then you have stress within the parasympathetic nervous system.

This is supposed to be the calming system. But instead of calmness, you may feel the heaviness of overwhelm and burden. Even in a depressed state, your body can be full of stress. The biochemistry and emotions behind stress in the parasympathetic nervous system can lead to fear and sadness that is difficult to overcome.

Maybe there is a fear of "what could or would happen" if you were to experience vitality. You may be fooled into thinking you are experiencing peace, but this is a false-calm. Inner conflict is causing your body to fight itself in an effort to be in a truly relaxed state. *Fear* of becoming anxious, *fear* of feeling emotions, and *fear* of overwhelm can be difficult to cope with. Also, being physically depleted of minerals, such as calcium, magnesium, and others could be a part of the equation.

The floating pause method allows a true calming of both the sympathetic and parasympathetic nervous systems. It is about enjoying "the wave" of life energy, just like being washed with the ocean's refreshing waves.

Settle into the pause gradually and smoothly. Allow yourself to release your fears and truly sink into the breath. Then, like the ocean wave, the energy will spread throughout your body. If you feel any lightheadedness, hesitation or a sense of tightness in your chest, shoulders, or head, that's okay. Keep sinking into the breath until you can do the floating pause breath with both inhalation and exhalation, without stress or concern, bringing yourself into a healing state of relaxation.

Let's practice.

Take a cleansing breath. Take a long inhale and a long exhale.

Now, inhale a long and slow breath.

When you reach the top of the breath, allow your breath to pause. If you feel a sense of urgency that is fine. *You have thousands of chances every day to practice over and over again.*

Now exhale slowly and at the end, pause and float your breath until you feel the natural inclination to calmly inhale the oxygen wave again.

Start to pay attention to any stress you might feel while breathing in either direction.

Notice how your desire to inhale is so automatic that you might have started to breath in ever so slightly before the floating pause. This hesitation could indicate a sense of apprehension Continue practicing the floating pause before you inhale.

It helps if you settle into your floating pause near the end of the exhalation. Recall the feeling when you were swinging at the playground. Re-create the anticipation of joy just before you arrive in the space of weightlessness.

The energy of this technique should be effortless. If you feel tightness or concern, practice until you experience calm and peace, with the swinging breath of the "floating pause."

The Double Exhale

The Double Exhale is a calm method for releasing stress from the "fight/flight" nervous system. You may use this technique instead of the forced exhale that is common with some breathing methods, as it is softer and more supportive. I have found that pain can be alleviated with this technique because when a person is focusing on the pain, there is a tendency to hold their breath and not let go.

When you exhale a portion of the breath it is entraining and educating your mind/body to release and receive with more responsibility and capacity.

Also, this technique allows for the possibility of releasing toxins from the respiratory system in a calm manner. With the forced breath, there is a release, but the energy of force might bring on additional resistance in the nervous system. This additional resistance gives the body one more thing to deal with.

The Double Exhale allows you to release another type of stress that might not have been fully released with the other procedures. I have found that the residual energy left at the "bottom of the bucket", so to speak, is heavier and difficult to access with most techniques. These could be thoughts, feelings and energy that need an extra boost to release. Using a forceful technique isn't always successful in moving this heavy energy. To use an analogy, the double exhale is similar to a pair of ocean waves. Often, the 2nd wave is stronger than the preceding one, and may reach farther onto the shoreline. Likewise, the 2nd part of the exhale causes a deeper cleansing effect within the person. It seems to encourage the lower part of the body to wake up.

The procedure is to exhale a small amount of air, and then continue with an additional short, easy exhale. At the end of this exhale, do a Floating Pause. Then fully inhale a relaxing breath.

Tightening the Muscles

An effective use of muscles, chakras and breath is the yogic technique of tightening the muscles in the lower half of the body during the breathing techniques. The three areas include:

Root Chakra (#1)   Coccyx/Anus area

Sacral Chakra (#2)   Lower Abdomen between the navel and the pubic bone (Lower Dan Tian)

Solar Plexus (#3)   Upper and Middle Abdomen between the navel and the rib cage

Each one of these areas will initiate different sensations and results. The Root Chakra area will allow for more release of past physical and emotional toxins. The Sacral Chakra, or Lower Dan Tian, will allow for resolution of inner conflict and physical relaxation of the intestines. The Solar Plexus area will allow for less worry, more trust and will increase absorption and digestion. All three will positively breach some of the cycles of addictions, problems with dissociation, being scattered, illness or unresolved emotions.

A client was releasing terror and fear issues, while dealing with physical constipation. She found that this technique, along with the centering breath-work, was highly beneficial. She first started with the

Sacral Chakra and the Solar Plexus separately and worked up to doing all three. She had been experiencing chronic constipation and chronic fear, but now she feels grounded and stable.

It is not wise to do all three simultaneously until each of them are individually practiced for several sessions.

The technique:

1. Take a deep cleansing breath.

2. Exhale any toxic feelings and thoughts with the double exhale breath.

3. Slow the breath to a calm breeze.

4. Focus on the desired area. (For example, on the Lower Dan Tian/Sacral chakra)

5. Take a deep breath in through the nostrils. Pause your breath (this is a floating pause).

6. Gently contract the muscles of the area (For example: the lower abdominal muscles).

7. Hold the contraction for at least 7 seconds.

8. Release the breath as if you are sending breath through the focused area. (For example: release the breath as if you are breathing through the lower abdominal region. The mouth will be releasing some air but the energy and muscle push will be through the Lower Dan Tian/Sacral Chakra).

9. Take another deep breath through the nostrils.

10. Breathe new life into the entire body.

11. Hold the Floating pause.

12. Focus on the desired area.

13. Tighten the muscles of the area.

14. Wait/Pause.

15. Release the breath as if you are breathing through the focused area.

16. Repeat at least 3 times. Or as many times as desired.

(Allow the breathing be light, floating, non-restrictive, and limit the muscle contractions to 5 to 7 pounds of pressure, at most.)

Suggestions: This technique is an advanced technique. Be sure to drink a lot of water before and after. Put your hands on the back near your kidneys if there is any pain in the body. Seek professional assistance if you get light-headed, dizzy or nauseated. Symptoms are rare if you are balanced physically, emotionally and spiritually. So, this is a good indicator, if you choose to see it that way.

For a deeper centering practice, and for pain release, this technique can be performed on any muscle or group of muscles.

Suzy was in constant pain after a surgery in the lower back region. She found that if she isolated certain muscles around the pain, tightened them with the breathing, released them gradually with the breath, that she was able to release localized pain. She also discovered that when she isolated muscles below the pain that she was able to move the pain down the body. She continued to isolate, tighten and release all the way down the body. Using this technique for concentration and focus is a power centering practice for full body awareness and mindfulness.

Abdominal Stretch and Relax

Often you are under stress without realizing it. So, try this. Focus on your abdomen. Is it tight? Are you holding it with some intensity? Did you realize you had tightness? In fact, do you think it is normal to have a tight abdomen? It may be popular to tighten up, but eventually the cost is more stress, more weight because food is not getting digested, anxiety and less sensitivity to spiritual energies. The goal is to maintain the optimal weight and still relax the abdomen. The benefits outweigh the alternative.

Practice during the day. Notice your abdominal region. Relax it spontaneously. Add one of the centering breath techniques and watch how fast you will be able to relax yourself in that area. Eventually relaxing the abdomen and deep breathing will become a habit.

Stretching and Centering

So many of the muscles and joints capture and hold physical and emotional blocks. It is possible that pain is just energy (physical and/or emotional) that has become blocked. This blocked energy causes additional stress that sometimes is hard to clear with just breathing and/or pills.

Stretching can assist you in clearing these blocks. Stretching can be done using the powerful techniques of yoga, Tai Chi, or Qigong, or with simple stretching.

Simple stretching basically involves the movement of the body, so that all or most of the muscles move from contraction to extension and back. Contraction is when the muscle is tightened up and is shorter. Extension is when the muscle is relaxed and stretched out longer. In other words, you want to contract your muscles, then stretch your muscles.

You can choose your own stretching methods or these simple ones. Notice clarity of mind and body when you do these stretches. Notice less body pain along with a deeper breath.

Legs Standing Side Stretch

1. Stand with your legs shoulder width apart.

2. Keep your feet facing forward.

3. Bend your knees so that from your eye view you only see the toenail portion of your feet.

4. Lean to the left until the left knee is past the left foot by an inch or two.

5. Lean to the right until the right knee is past the right foot by an inch or two.

6. Lean back and forth several times.

7. Combine the technique with slow breaths.

8. Breathe out slowly when you move. Breathe in when you pause the movement.

This will stretch the muscles in the legs and hips including: adductors, the tensor fascia lata, gluteus medius, gluteus maximus, peroneus, the tibials, and the quadratus lumborum. Physically this will help the body release toxins. Emotionally it will help release deep suppressed emotions and traumas. Denial can be found in the lower torso and leg muscles. Traumas of the past are often stored there because the pain of abuse or other overwhelming situations are so confusing to the mind and heart at the time the events occurred.

Justification for the storage of emotional trauma and subsequent denial does not take the pain and associated body and spiritual sabotages away. Only by moving the memories out and through the body will it be able to leave. Either use centering breath and stretch techniques to help move the old memories or try some of the following: Massage, Energy Kinesiology, emotional processing, yoga, or tai chi.

Torso Rotation Stretch

1. Stand with your legs shoulder-width apart.

2. Keep your feet facing forward.

3. Bring both arms straight out in front of your body.

4. Swing the arms around towards the left until the right arm is over the chest, the left arm is stretched behind the body and the body is twisted as far as comfortable to the left.

5. Make sure your eyes follow the left hand behind the body so that the head flows with the stretch.

6. Swing the arms around towards the right until the left arm is over the chest, the right arm is stretched behind the body and the body is twisted as far as comfortable to the right.

7. Make sure your eyes follow the right hand behind the body so that the head flows with the stretch.

8. Swing the arms and twist the body to the left.

9. Swing the arms and twist the body to the right.

10. Swing and stretch several times. More than 15.

This will stretch the muscles of the torso, shoulders and neck. This includes the abdominal muscles, the rhomboids, latissimus dorsi, trapezius muscles, etc.

Advanced: Point the palms of your hands towards the direction of the motion. The energy flow will increase.

Neck Stretch

So many burdens of the world weigh heavily on the shoulders and neck. The amount of information that goes through the neck is already enormous. When you add the tremendous pressure of unresolved emotional and physical issues the neck tightens and can contribute to hypertension and other physical and emotional problems.

You could be so disconnected from both feeling and sensing your body, that real peace and joy is far from you. So, to find peace - open the bottle "neck".

Circle neck stretch technique

1. Flex the neck to the left, with the ear toward the left shoulder.

2. Rotate the head, chin to chest and continue until the neck is flexed toward the right shoulder.

3. Continue the rotation, moving in a circle by extending the head toward the back, until the neck is flexed to the left again, stretching as you rotate.

4. Rotate the head several times clockwise.

5. Rotate the head several times counter-clockwise.

6. Rotating slowly, while softly breathing assists in releasing.

7. Release the emotional tensions that get stuck in the neck area.

Feel the joints of the neck and let them release the daily beliefs and frustrations that have burdened you. Feel the neck muscles start to loosen. Let the blood flow, the lymph move, and the nutrients assimilate throughout the head and the body.

Open the mind to connect to the body. Feel yourself become one. Feel the energy of connecting to your whole body down to the feet.

Vector Neck Stretch

1. Sit or stand straight so that the back and neck are in proper posture.

2. Turn the head 35 degrees towards the left so that the nose is pointing left.

3. Move the head down towards the chest bringing the chin to the left collar-bone.

4. Raise your chin and diagonally swing the head back.

5. Do this movement several times.

6. Reposition the head and turn the head 35 degrees towards the right so that the nose is pointing right.

7. Move the head down towards the chest bringing the chin to the right collar-bone.

8. Raise your chin and diagonally swing the head back.

9. Do this several times.

This technique helps the neck and the coccyx (tailbone and lower back). Symptoms such as headaches may clear with this technique.

Taking responsibility for your life and choosing to let others to take responsibility for theirs, while letting go of what you cannot change, really assists in relieving neck and shoulder pain.

Combining the Breath and Stretch

As you do the stretching, slow down the stretch and use the breath to create a full release. Every time you move out and away from standing straight and your center, breathe out.

Each time you come back to center, breathe in. The movement of the stretch will slow down and the breath will be deep and from the abdomen. Focus the breath toward your feet, or on the Lower Dan Tian.

When there is pain in a muscle area, the following advanced breathing stretch is very effective.

Isolate the area that needs support. Find a muscle movement area where the pain is located that will help release the energy that is stuck and causing problems. Use the breathing technique with the movement as described in this section.

If you experience pain with the stretch, be sure that you are breathing out with the movement.

Movement is required to distribute the fullness of energy in the body. Without appropriate motion, oxygen cannot be distributed to the right place at the right time. Toxins waiting to be expelled cannot be expelled, and emotional stress tightens the muscles, causing pain.

The stretching technique is powerful because the body will physically start to release toxins, such as built-up lactic acid, and the body will move the toxins out of the muscles and through the lymphatic system to be expelled. The body receives support in processing the toxins, because the breath gives the body energy at the cellular level at the time of release.

You can combine different stretches, breaths and imagery to enhance your experience. An advanced form of *Breath and Stretch* is to focus on an emotional stress in your life and breathe it out. Breathe in life and renew. Be creative. Be alive. Choose to live instead of choosing the slow death of denial, negative feelings or destructive thoughts. Each moment is a gift.

Advanced Stretching and Breath Technique

1. Take a cleansing breath.

2. Breathe out.

3. Breathe in and pause with a floating pause.

4. Move into the stretch until slight discomfort arises.

5. Hold

6. Breathe out slowly for the count of at least 7 seconds.

7. Breathe in while relaxing the muscles.

8. Hold

9. Move back into the stretch and tighten the muscles.

10. Breath out slowly to a count of 7 as you release the muscles.

11. Repeat six more times.

12. After a total of 7 repetitions, go deeper into the stretch until slight discomfort arises.

13. Hold

14. Breathe out slowly for 7 seconds.

15. Breathe in while relaxing the position of the muscle.

16. Hold.

17. Go to the new position again and breathe out slowly for 7 seconds.

18. Continue this process until you have the full range of motion for the muscle you are working on.

19. Drink water, and make sure you eat plenty of green leafy vegetables if you do this technique.

Add the Isometric aspect by providing a resistance to the muscle. This increases muscle release, muscle strength, toxic release, and centering effectiveness.

Cranial & Spine Breath & Stretch

The spine and the cranial area of the body contain the fluid identified as the cerebral spinal fluid. This fluid is like the information river to the ventricles of the brain and the spine. Inhibiting its flow can result in headaches, pain, sluggishness, and even possible digestive issues. Cerebral Spinal Fluid (CSF) is constantly being produced and eventually is pushed into the lymph system of the body. Spiritually it can affect the energy of the chakras and other energy centers of the body.

This technique is important for Life Centering and grounding. It honors the spinal support system and the central nervous system. Most individuals desperately need this technique due to the stresses they create in their life. Supporting the CSF flow will support your flow through life.

1. Lie down.

2. Take a cleansing breath.

3. Breathe in as you stretch your neck by moving your chin in the air and moving your head backwards.

4. Breathe out as you move your head and chin forward to the chest. Keep your head on the bed/couch.

5. Repeat by breathing in as you move your head back and chin up.

6. Breathe out as you move your head down.

7. Now include the feet.

8. As you move your head back – point your feet and toes away from your body.

9. As you move your head down to the chest – flex your feet and toes towards the body. (The idea is to get the spine to stretch).

10. Repeat. Breathe in as you point your head back and away as you move your feet and toes away.

11. Breathe out as you point your head and chin towards the chest and your feet and toes stretch towards the head.

12. Do this procedure at least 12 times, once a day. (doing this more often will provide extra calming effects.)

This technique was taught to me by the Loomis Institute and my wife immediately incorporated into her life. She seldom has any neck aches due to this procedure.

Let the pulse of life resonate

CHAPTER NINE

Centering with Movement

There are empowering possibilities when you combine movement with centering techniques. These possibilities can affect all levels of your existence, from getting the needed oxygen and nutritional fuel to your cells in a calm balanced delivery method to connecting spiritually to the world around you. The cells are very reactive to the state of the heart and mind.

If the mind and heart are worried, angry or anxious, the sympathetic nervous system is on alert and the parasympathetic nervous system is put on hold. Thus, the release of metabolic and other toxins is halted and they remain in the cells, not leaving space for nutrients. The cells do not want to receive nutrients if there is danger.

Centered Exercises

When you exercise, the cellular metabolic activity is at its prime for the release of toxins, and if you are centered while doing physical activity, the release is more balanced, safe, deep and complete. The mind opens up and can be more available for mental and spiritual enlightenment and awareness.

Melissa is a beautiful young lady who enjoyed wearing clothing that highlighted her blond flowing hair and smooth, long legs. She smiled with innocence but her eyes showed some longing and a little discontent. She had a strong compulsive behavior of excessive exercising to maintain a façade. The image she had created was a paper-thin model that was not possible physically. Her compulsion made her run and workout six hours a day. Her eating patterns matched her obsession. She ate very little meat, subsisting mainly on green salads. Her doctor was extremely concerned, watching the anorexic activity that was taking her into a negative spiral that would be hard to survive.

She exercised with intensity of resentment. While she ran, she not only thought of her goal of being the perfect shape, she was also filled with negative thoughts towards her father, mother, an abuser, and to life. These negative emotions and thoughts were driving her to keep the intensity up and growing. She needed to work through those negative factors and to start exercising with emotions and thoughts that were positive.

The intensity of negative self-talk and destructive emotions is much greater with the pounding of physical activity. The negativity is driven deep into the cellular memory and is much more abusive to the body than physically passive mental and emotional activity.

Melissa needed to re-center herself before and during her physical activity. Then, she not only could stop the downward spiral, but also reverse it. Her family thought that the mind had nothing to do with her problem. They thought she should stop exercising immediately, be forced to perform calmer activities and eat more balanced meals. The possibility was, if she stopped abruptly, she could collapse.

As Melissa centered with breathing, emotional processing, mental imagery and exercise, she was able to gradually change her lifestyle and deal with her compulsive, physical behavior. It became easier because the centered physical activity helped her integrate with her the body much faster than if she had stopped. Melissa was able to empower herself mentally, physically and spiritually.

Use some of the following exercises to assist you incorporating centering and integrating the physical body with the mind and heart.

Centered Walking

The author is in favor of assertive walking over too aggressively running. It seems to be more balanced and easier on the body. There are reports that it is also easier on the heart. Also, the body creates more free radicals when aggressive exercise is continued over long periods of time.

Combine assertive walking with centered directed breathing. Encourage your mind to create a powerful environment for mindful, spiritual experiences, emotional release, satisfaction, mental resolution and clarity. Combine this with physical cleansing and building. Centered walking will provide a new, whole-body centering experience.

Centered Hiking

Very much like centered walking, with the focus on the energies and stimulus of nature. Whether in the plushness of greenery and watery mists, or in the dryness and stability of rocks, centered walking is a deeply effectual tool for the quest of wholeness.

The author has noted that with the rejuvenation of the body, time becomes almost non-existent in the centered hiking experience. It feels surreal when the mind surrenders and the union of self with the energies of nature flow with one another. Its as if nature is supporting the movement and moving the body forward. There is a sensation of a hundred hands clapping, without sound, praising the natural union, as nature wants communion with the human child that is often prodigal.

Perform centered hiking in similar way to centered walking—with the intent to understand trees, plants and animals. Make the experience a sensory one – touch, energetic sense, smell, see, hear, intuit, taste, etc.

Cross Crawls

This method is very good for brain integration and coordination. Take your left hand and touch your raised right knee. Touch the tail bone with your right hand. Return the leg and arms. Now lift the left knee and touch it with your right hand while your left hand is touching your tailbone. Move slowly.

This time-tested technique has been popularized by Brain Gym by Paul Dennison. In occupational therapy, it is called cross patterning. It is a highly effective, proven technique suitable for all ages.

When combined with deep breathing and focused centering techniques, cross crawling becomes a great way to deeply connect your mind, brain stem, hip proprioceptor sites and the left and right brain. It physically provides more oxygen to the brain cross laterally, and spiritually connects those same areas. There is an increased connection of the brain to the pericardium, heart and limbic system.

Go slowly with your breath and movement. Enhance the experience by moving the eyes in rotation and blinking. To increase the experience, affirmations reviewed in the mind and feelings experienced in the heart can create an abundance of health in physical, emotional and spiritual levels.

Valerie Moreton's affirmation for the cross crawl is "I take responsibility for my life." The author adds any of the following:

I integrate, focus, and enjoy taking responsibility for my life.

I respond maturely to life and its vast experiences.

I enjoy the challenges of responding responsibly to life.

I learn with each experience and grow-up all parts of myself.

I focus clearly.

Other movements that are centering include:

Side to side jumping jacks – this is where the left leg is lifted to the side and the left hand reaches to touch the left leg. The right hand is raised laterally (to the side) up in the air. The sequence reverses with the right leg lifted laterally (to the side) with the right hand touching the right leg. The left hand is raised laterally up in the air. The affirmation for this movement is "I let go, relax, and trust every moment."

Additional affirmations:

I left 'stress' at its' trap door today.

I take on the challenge to see how I 'flow' through my day.

I turn worry and concern into curiosity and wisdom.

My energy is balanced with vitality and strength.

Mountain Trainer – bring the right hand to the front of the body and stretch out the right arm to the front. Place the right foot behind the body. Place the left foot in front of the body and the left arm towards the back of the body. Now switch places: the right leg is placed in front of the body and the right arm is placed to the back. The left leg is placed in the back and the left arm is raised to the front of the body. Valerie Moreton's affirmation for this movement is "I let go of the past and make room for beneficial change."

The author adds: "I move out pain, suffering, hatred and blame, and make room for life, love, strength, and joy."

Additional affirmations:

I enjoy managing life in all aspects, surprises and daily routines.

The past is a teacher, the future is novel, the present is the creative fun of managing the moment.

I am releasing the clutter of life and embracing the clarity of expressing myself fully in life.

Lean to – stand up facing a wall. The distance from the wall is at arm's length. Put your hands down to the side. The arms should be loose because the arms and hands will stop the fall. Lean towards the wall slowing and before the body touches the wall, catch yourself with your hands against the wall. Now breathe out gradually while pushing slowly away from the wall.

The procedure of catching the fall when you lean towards the wall initiates a fear response. The gradual and slow centering breath after catching oneself is the release of fear and replacing it with calm, peace, and grounding connection to self and life. This helps with scattered feelings, fear, finding personal space, giving, taking, and other boundaries.

This is fantastic to assist aggressive children who push people away, and for recessive children who withdraw and do not set boundaries.

The affirmations can be any of the following:

I trust life.

I know my boundaries and I am safe.

I communicate love and respect.

I am respected by others and communicate openly.

Stay present in your body, stay present in your life.

CHAPTER TEN

Centering Practices

A centered life is a mindful life. We can elevate the simplest routines and habits of daily living when we perform them with focus, attention and centeredness. When you brush your teeth, eat an apple, walk across the room, look into another person's eyes, listen to the rain, read a book, talk on the telephone or take a breath – each action can be a celebration of life and living. Each action is a gift.

Each gift of action is an opportunity to bring integration and congruency to your life. In the book *Siddhartha* by Herman Hesse, the main character started his quest for truth perplexed by his master's focus on carrying water and chopping wood like everyone else. Siddhartha thought that his master had achieved a status that required others to be like slaves of the master. Undaunted by the student, the master continued on the daily task and continued finding joy where most never do. There is a whole universe within a grain of sand, a feather, a thought or a task. Take the opportunity to find your unique experience of joy in the daily routine and habit.

Centered Journaling

In order to greatly enhance your centering experiences, take the time to write. While you are connected at many levels of emotion, spirit and body; the insights that come are pure, clear, simple and life changing. Most of those insights eventually fade because the stressful life cannot hold that pure energy. So, take the time to write and journal. The author is particularly impressed with the Artist's Way program of daily letters, or the program called the Gratitude Journal.

Often people do not write because of lack of time. Some hold deep-seated sabotages, such as the fear of exposure, fear of seeing the truth, failure, success or fear of experiencing old emotions. Instead of allowing the emotional or mental blocks to rule and control, face your fear through writing. Allow yourself to release those blocks and process with the written word. Deep feelings and thoughts hold many of the keys and clues to your desires to be at peace, calm and centered.

Technique:

1. Do one of the centering techniques before writing.

2. While writing notice your breath.

3. Spontaneously write without editing.

4. When the hands have stopped writing spontaneously more than two times, stop.

5. Review what you wrote.

6. Do a deep imagery Centering meditation on your written words and let the words teach you wisdom and understanding.

7. Write once a week or once a month, and watch for patterns for deeper messages.

Journaling can capture the energy of the moment. Writing, like art, holds the energy of the moment forever. Enjoy going back several months later to certain writings and savoring the energy that was experienced while writing those pieces.

Centered Sharing

Terry was so worried about her health that she consumed too many supplements a day. The amount of supplement consumption was probably contributing to her illnesses rather than healing her. Terry was introduced to the idea of reducing the supplements and replacing them with love. She was confused. She thought more was better. The author offered the idea of the sharing of herself, as a healing path.

She could volunteer or get involved in assisting others, including children, teenagers or adults. By sharing herself, the number of supplements needed could decrease and more importantly the assimilation of the supplements would increase. She could not see the connection and refused to see or understand the concept. Unfortunately, she remained in constant pain.

A couple of years later this story was told to another client that was on the edge of death due to massive surgeries and complications. She took the story to heart and gradually started to spend a few hours each week sharing and coaching others with their emotional issues. Even though she was very weak, she noticed major energy bursts and changes. She still has some complications, but her body has less pain and she is full of life and hope.

Centered sharing is simply the act of sending and sharing the light within so that another can sense the light they already possess. It is sharing the joy one-to-one and asking others to do likewise. Forgive others and yourself. Remember that everyone is blessed with God's love and center yourself to that gift.

This is a simple, yet misunderstood concept. Most sharing is done with an agenda. Compare these two scenarios: a) sharing once a week while worrying what others think, doing it for a reward, doing it for status, doing it to get God's approval or any other questionable reason; b) sharing once a week with deep centered awareness, with the intent to increase the flow of life and love on the earth, and to give the fruit of joy to others. The results are amazing when step "b" is practiced and shared.

Centered Ceremonies

Ceremonies, rituals, routines and religious rites can be powerful tools for healing. Originally, ceremonies or rituals were instituted to teach, to remind, and to connect individuals to principles, values and to God. Often the original intent is forgotten and more value is placed on the ritual than on the purpose. But do not let that stop you from honoring your true self through ceremonies.

Create focused ceremonies that include centering yourself to the divine within and to God. Doing this can bring deep wisdom and healing. Do you have family ceremonies or traditions that bring your family and friends together? Do you have a ceremony, ritual, routine or religious activity that brings spiritual awareness and deep inward introspection? Either use an established ceremony or create a new one to open the connection of body, mind and soul.

Technique:

1. Find or create a ceremony that you feel can assist in your path of centering.

2. Do deep centering breathing while in the process of the ceremony.

3. Watch the changes in your body, mind, heart and essence.

4. Listen deeply for understanding and wisdom.

5. Send out the intent that the ceremony continues energetically during the day and week.

6. Send out gratitude for the opportunity of deep spiritual process and connection.

7. Journal your experience and awareness.

When you start to understand the deeper meaning and purpose of the ceremony you will start to receive insights during the day while doing other tasks.

Wisdom is not in the words, but in the message behind the words. Music is not in the notes, but in the resonance between the notes. Understanding is not in the knowledge but in the awakening of awe. Knowingness is not the data but a state of beingness where you glimpse a moment of eternity.

Vibrations of the universe can and do come in any and all forms of frequencies. Fast, slow, high and low. If you are open, you will become coherent and resonant with many of those vibrations, sensations, and awakenings. Judgment blocks the path. Gratitude, curiosity and child-like awe open the doors.

Completion

Coming Home to yourself is vital. Too often, people go off in search of self, trying to forget about that which they have come from. Even if you do not know all things and have not experienced the bliss you want, still Come Home often to reconnect, regroup and then start again. To throw away all your past and your values in search of the new, is unwise. To shift yourself, and add to what you have or know is wiser and more complete.

The centering methods in this book are meant to bring you back to your true self. Until you find that, take it a step at a time.

The truth of who you truly are will surface gradually and more completely.

Remember to surrender, breathe, let go and invite in joy, laughter, respect, honor and gratitude.

Return to center and enjoy the silence within.

GLOSSARY

Alignment *is a synchronization of the energy patterns of the mind, heart, body and soul.* It is like the harmonizing of a song. The mind, heart, body, and soul each carry a unique energy pattern, or frequency. When they are synchronized, the multiple notes create harmony. When there is disharmony there is a misalignment, leading to internal confusion, or chaos. The act of centering allows conflicting beliefs, emotions, and memories to shift out of chaos and into congruency, bringing the person into a state where their energy can flow. This allows the individual to obtain a state of healing and oneness. Alignment allows a person to achieve optimal energy levels, as the entire system is working together. Living in disharmony and chaos requires the expenditure of energy to maintain the misaligned state.

Attuning – *Tuning the chaos and randomness of the mind, heart, and body into a symphony that is blended and harmonious.* Opposing, or incongruent emotions and beliefs leads to internal conflict. Conflict can give rise to discomfort, illness, and emotional upset. Attuning brings into account the various agendas within an individual. Centering helps the body integrate the many parts of the Self into a harmonious state of Wholeness.

Centered Breathing – *Breathing, moving, and meditating that assists you in creating congruency and alignment of the mind, heart, body, and soul.* The purpose of centered breathing is to focus the attention of the mind to the act of breathing, and away from the clutter of thoughts and distractions. Centered Breathing increases oxygen and flow throughout the body and activates the parasympathetic nervous system. This is the state of healing, and the way to align all the aspects of the Core Self.

Centering – *The action of alignment and integration of the mind, heart, body, and soul into a cohesive and flowing experience and State of Being.* The result of centering is a connection to the inner most parts of the Self so that the mind, heart, body, and soul are on the same path without internal conflict. Being centered feels like a calm river of energy flowing through the body, enlivening the soul, and connecting the heavens above to the earth below. When you are Centered, you are connected to your authentic Self, while also feeling connected to all other parts of the universe. It is a state of calm happiness. It is a place of Stillness. It is an "inner knowing."

Conflict – *The opposite of centering.* Conflict is the result of the mind, heart, and body manifesting different agendas and beliefs. It is as if different parts of your Self are at war and oppose each other. Conflict can manifest as explosive emotions or suppressed feelings that lead to confusion, frustration, anxiety, depression, illness, and/or disconnection with Self or others.

Congruency *is a synchronization of the intentions and beliefs of the mind, heart, body and soul.* Often, there is a disagreement within a person's own system. The mind may think one way, but the emotions and/or body hold a different belief. This is the cause of many unexplained headaches, emotions, aches and pains. When a person is congruent with their belief and purpose, they are in alignment. Congruency of the heart, mind, body, and soul aligns the person's energy into synchronized patterns. This allows the whole Self to align to the same purpose, direction, and path.

The Double Exhale *is a calm method for releasing stress from the "fight/flight" nervous system.* You may use this technique instead of the forced exhale that is common with some breathing methods, as it is softer and more supportive. The procedure is to exhale a small amount of air, and then continue with an additional short, easy exhale. At the end of this exhale, do a Floating Pause. Then fully inhale a relaxing breath.

Floating Pause – *A gentle holding breath that is non-restrictive, nonforceful.* It is like taking a pause. For example, take a long breath in. Now, at the top, pause with a floating hold of the breath, like being on a swing, when your body floats for a second at the top and everything seems to be on pause. Then release naturally and allow your body, heart, mind, and soul to be integrated together.

Core Self – *A "still point", a quiet and peaceful state of being.* The Core Self is an active and alive state, although it is not an emotion, an object, an accomplishment, or an attitude. This centered state of Being is grounded in clarity, oneness, peace, strength, and confidence.

Grounding – *A connection to the earth that is physical, emotional, mental, and spiritual.* A tree needs its roots to be well established in the earth so that the rest of the tree can be abundant and thrive in the environment. Roots that are well grounded can feed the rest of the tree, and likewise, be fed. Like a tree, we receive energy and nurturance from the Earth. To be properly grounded the whole tree, and the whole person, needs to be aligned. The centering and aligning of all parts of the tree, or the person, to one energy pattern and purpose, assists in grounding through the roots as well as with the source of life energy. All bodies can experience the profound sense of life-force or the source of energy. It flows deep within and is facilitated with grounding and centering.

Heart –*Through the Heart we connect to ourselves as well as to others.* The heart has different aspects: physical, emotional, mental and spiritual and energetic. The *physical heart* is vital to our physical existence, as it not only pumps the blood, but reads the blood to monitor our requirements. The *emotional heart* can break, and it can heal. The *mental heart* can influence your mind and can give you passion to live in each and every moment. The *spiritual heart* is close to God and the purpose of life and sharing. The *chakra heart* is an energy center that connects the unseen energy around us with the nerves and the brain. The *brain heart* is found on the right side of the brain, and is emotional and fluid in its processing, a place of dreams and music. The heart is an essential part of all aspects of life. Opening the closed heart creates great joy and may be repeated often until the centered heart chooses to remain in this more spontaneous way of living.

Heart/Body - *The connection between the Heart and the Body bridges the emotions with the sensations of the organs and tissues of the body.* The body has reactions that show up as physical pain, tightness or organ functions or dysfunctions. When the emotions and the sensory feelings are flowing or working together then the heart and body adjust to the stresses of life with greater ease. There are always daily stresses. Addressing those stresses so that the body doesn't not over-react with tight shoulders, hives, organ problems and more is the best and most centered way. The body has bio-alarms that are reflections of the stress of the heart and mind. Centering the heart with the body allows the body to release the alarms in a way that is calm and efficient.

Knowingness – *An internal awareness.* A Knowing is a clear, intuitive observation of an understanding that comes without force or computation. It is simply an awareness of what is and what is not. When a person is centered, Knowingness or Knowing is easy and clear. Knowingness can come at any time, but to facilitate a deeper insightful state, seek to be centered and aligned internally. Knowingness allows you to attune your inner parts so that the information coming from the Core Self and the universe is concise and authentic, and of course, valid. Knowingness is a state of trust.

Mind/Body - *The connection between the Mind and the Body bridges logic with the sensations of the tissues of the body and the organs.* When the stress of life builds up and the mind is trying to force solutions, the body will react with tightness, fatigue, overwhelm, rapid heart, and many other possibilities. The body will listen to your stress messages and react. What you need to do is listen to your body. It is speaking loudly and the mind needs to pay attention. Use Life Centering breathing and meditation techniques to calmly bridge the mind and the body.

Mind/Heart - *The connection between the Mind and the Heart bridges logic with emotions, the analytical and the spatial, the rigid and the flowing, work and fun, details and the big picture.* It allows for a complete experience, because life is not just logic nor is it only emotions. For example, a sporting event requires rules and boundaries, and the players need to put their whole heart into their performance. Thus, the game is enjoyable when there is a synergy between the planned action and the emotional zeal from the players and the spectators. This example can apply to all areas of life, including, school, work, health, and personal relationships.

Mudras –*Hand or body positions that can hold and carry information.* Mudras are commonly used in yoga as well as in Energy Kinesiology. As demonstrated by the posture, body positions convey the state of a person. For example, sadness is displayed by holding the shoulders forward with the torso slumped, while feelings of confidence and courage are displayed with the shoulders back, the head upright and the torso straight. Hand mudras employ the placement of fingers and thumb in various positions. Each finger placement, as well as each postural position carries a specific piece of information, which is conveyed through the nervous system to the brain, the chakras, and other energy systems, supporting the emotions and body's energy fields. You can enhance centering with the use of mudras.

Navel – *The naval was the portal for nourishment while in the womb and continues to be a place for energy nourishment.* The navel is located in a central place in the human body. The naval carries great significance in Eastern Medicine. It is a bridge for the yin and yang, the opposing energies of the body. The navel is close to the lower "Dantian", a power center addressed by practitioners of Qi Gong, and holds strong life-force of energy in the lower portion of the body. The navel bridges this Dantian energy with the energy in the solar plexus and sacral chakra fields. It is one of the representations of Center.

Self-talk - *The mental feedback that a person gives themselves throughout the day.* It is automatic and spontaneous. Often self-talk can be negative and destructive. Other times, it can be productive and supportive. It usually reflects the state of a person's inner world. When you are confident and calm, the self-talk tends to support that. When you are upset, angry, fearful, or lacking in self-confidence, then self-talk reflects negativity toward self or others. Authentic inner communication is powerful and uplifting. It opens an individual to new insights and awareness. Destructive self-talk creates mental ruts, shuts the truth down and negatively filters your view of life and others. "If-only", or "I wish" self-talk provides justifications for a person to live in a fantasy that does not have a happy ending.

Source of energy – *The life-force energy that flows from nature.* This is known by many names, such as chi/qi, Ki, or prana. Every being inherits this energy at birth which fuels us until death. In the natural sciences of Eastern philosophy, there are several types of source energy that are identified. Source energy comes from parents, and is also derived from air, from food, from earth, and from heaven. Excess stress and misalignment of energy uses up source energy too quickly. Centering helps the body conserve this precious life-force or source of energy. Breathing in a centered way, or eating in a centered manner, improves the quality of life-force from the air and food so that the body can use it without difficulty, thus super-charging the body with energy. When you center to your core-self, to a still point, you can experience the magnitude of the original chi/qi or inherited life force and source energy. It is real, authentic, and truly precious.

Wholeness *is a Centered state where there is an alignment of the mind, heart, body, and soul.* The state of Wholeness brings with it a calm, natural flow and connectedness to one's own energy fields. Wholeness attracts spontaneous living and joy. This state of alignment relies on a matrix of communication between all parts and all dimensions of a person, simultaneously communicating and creating one beautiful symphony. A transformation into Wholeness brings all things into One, like a universe inside one's Self.

BIBLIOGRAPHY

Acu-Yoga, Michael Reed Gach with Carolyn Marco, Tokyo: Japan Publications, 1981.

Affective Neuroscience, Jaak Pankseep, New York, NY: Oxford University Press, 1998.

Anatomy of the Spirit, Caroline Myss, PhD., New York: Harmony Books division of Crown Publishers of Random House, 1996.

Artist's Way, Julia Cameron, New York, NY: Tarcher/Putnum Publishing, 1992.

The Body is the Barometer of the Soul, Annette Noontil, Victoria, Australia: Gemcraft P/L Dist., 1994.

Chinese Medicine for Maximum Immunity, Jason Elias and Katherine Ketcham, New York: Three Rivers Press, 1998.

Cognitive Neuroscience of Emotion, Richard D. Lane and Lynn Nadel, New York, NY: Oxford University Press, 2000.

Descartes' Error: Emotion, Reason, and the Human Brain, A.R. Damasio, New York, NY: G.P Putnum's Sons, 1994.

DMT, the Spirit Molecule, Rick Strassman, MD, Rochester, Vermont: Inner Traditions International, 2001.

Dr. Andrew Weil's Self-Healing, Andrew Weil, Watertown, MA: Thorne Communications, Inc., Feb. 2001, Oct. 2001.

The Energy of Money, Maria Nemeth, Phd., New York, NY: The Ballantine Publishing Group, 1999.

Eastern Body Western Mind, Anodea Judith, Berkeley, CA: Celestial Arts, 1996.

Energy Medicine in Therapeutics and Human Performance, James Oschman, Philadelphia, PA: Butterworth Heinemann, 2003.

Enzymes, The Key to Health, Howard F. Loomis, D.C., F.I.A.C.A., Madison, WI: 21st Century Nutrition Publishing, 1999.

Feelings Buried Alive Never Die, Karol K. Truman, Phoenix, AZ: Olympus Pub., 2003.

Heal the Cause, Valerie Seeman Moreton, ND, San Diego, CA: Kalos Pub., 1996.

The Heartmath Solution, Doc Childre and Howard Martin, New York, NY: HarperCollins Pub., 1999.

Integration of Dynamic and Postural Reflexes into Whole Body Movement System, Svetlana Masgutova, N. Akhmatova, S. Goncharova, Moscow, Russia: Ascension Private Educational Institute of Psychological and Edu-K Assistance, 1998.

Kinergetics, Philip Rafferty, Ormond, Victoria, Australia, 2000.

Light Years Ahead, Brian J. Breiling, Ph.D., Tiburon, CA: Light Years Ahead Productions, 1996.

Loving What Is, Byron Katie, New York, NY: Harmony Books, 2002.

Meditation As Medicine, Dharma Singh Khalsa, M.D. and Cameron Stauth, New York, NY: Pocket Books, Simon & Schuster, 2001.

Bibliography

Messages from Water, Dr. Masaru Emoto, Tokyo, Japan: I.H.M. General Research Institute, Hado Kyoilusha Co.,Ltd., 2003.

Mind Map, Your Guide to Prosperity and Fulfillment, Sanford Frumker, University Heights, Ohio: Health Associates, 1994.

Molecules of Emotion, Candance Pert, New York: Simon and Schuster, 1997.

Neuro-Acupuncture, Cho, Z.H., Wong, E.K., Fallon, J., Los Angeles, CA: Q-Puncture, Inc., 2001.

Neuro Emotional Pathways Books 1, 2, 3, Hugo Tobar, Murwillumbah, Australia: Mt. Warning Kinesiology, 2003.

Nutritional Influences on Estrogen Metabolism, Douglas C. Hall, M.D., Applied Nutritional Science Reports, Advanced Nutrition Publications, Inc., 2001.

The Power of Personal Health, Jack Schwarz, New York, NY: Penguin Group, 1992.

Power versus Force, David R. Hawkins, M.D., Sedona, AZ: Veritas Publishing, 1998.

Professional Kinesiology Practice, Dr. Bruce and Joan Dewe, Auckland, NZ: Professional Health Publications, 2000.

Psychoneuroimmunoendocrinology article, Robert A Anderson, MD, Townsend, WA: *Townsend Letter for Doctors and Patients*, Feb/Mar 2001.

A Revolutionary Way of Thinking, Dr. Charles Krebs, Melbourne, Australia: Hill of Content Publishing, 1998.

The Root of Chinese Qigong, Dr. Yang, Jwing-Ming, Roslindale, MA: YMAA Publications Center, 1997.

Siddhartha, Herman Hesse, New York, NY: New Directions, 1951.

The Sivananda Companion to Yoga, Lidell, Lucy, with Narayani and Giris Rabinovitch, New York: Simon and Schuster, Inc., 1983.

Synaptic Self, Joseph LeDoux, New York, NY: Penguin Group, 2002

Tao Te Ching, Lao Tzu, New York, NY: Bantam Books, 1990.

Vibrational Medicine, Richard Gerber, M.D., Santa Fe, New Mexico: Bear and Company, 1988.

You Can Heal Your Life, Louise L. Hay, Carson, CA: Hay House, 1987.

You Can't Afford the Luxury of a Negative Thought, John-Roger and Peter McWilliams, Los Angeles, CA: Prelude Press, 1991.

ABOUT THE AUTHOR

Ronald Wayman

For almost 30 years, Ron has dedicated his life to coaching individuals in achieving the desires of their hearts through empowerment and congruency of the heart, mind, body and soul as a Neuro-Energy Kinesiologist, a Certified Food Enzyme Consultant and an Empowerlife Emotional Coach.

Ron enjoys teaching the Life Centering techniques to assist his family, friends, and clients. He founded the Sensory Dynamics Center, and Empowerlife Kinesiology: a Body & Mind energy school; and co-founded Live by Heart, LLC, a coaching school for living by heart/mind/body.

Ron's expansive work incorporates breakthroughs in brain-neuroscience, nutrition, body energy systems, sensory integration, focused emotional processing and motivational heart-mind empowerment. He is continually developing new techniques for working with the energy systems of the body, based upon traditional Chinese methodologies.

These restructured and original tools assist the practitioner to experience and facilitate tremendous physical, emotional and energetic alchemy.

His current creative passions include writing and developing the Live by Heart program, with his partner, Jennifer Marie.

Ron and his wife, Janette, are the parents of six children, and proud grandparents to 13. They reside in West Jordan, Utah.

For more information about classes and trainings, email us at info@ livebyheart.net or visit livebyheart.net, or empowerlifekinesiology. com.

Made in the USA
San Bernardino, CA
21 January 2020